Patricia was born in Birmingham and moved to London when she was nine, and was educated there. She studied with the Open University while in her forties, gaining a BSc covering various subjects in health and social care, psychology and philosophy.

Patricia has worked in finance and has been a carer and a support worker for children with learning differences. She is a Reiki Master and an advanced Theta healer. She is clairaudient and clairsentient, writes letters, and individual soul readings for healing and guidance.

She is married, has two sons and lives in Kent. She loves travelling and reading, adores elephants and enjoys a good 'whodunnit' drama.

This book is dedicated to Robert, Jamie and Alasdair.
Thank you for all we have shared together.

Patricia McDowall

50 LETTERS FROM SPIRIT

A Call to Awaken

AUSTIN MACAULEY PUBLISHERS™

LONDON • CAMBRIDGE • NEW YORK • SHARJAH

A CIP catalogue record for this title is available from the British Library.

ISBN 9781786939258 (Paperback)
ISBN 9781786939265 (E-Book)

www.austinmacauley.com

First Published (2018)
Austin Macauley Publishers Ltd.
25 Canada Square
Canary Wharf
London
E14 5LQ

Acknowledgements

With grateful thanks to Marsilio, my spiritual guide. I hope I am a worthy messenger.

Thank you to my wonderful friends: Karen, Kaushala and Lin.

To Karen, my soul sister, thank you for your love and support over the years in all matters spiritual and here on the earth plane. For your deep understanding of who I am. For all the dashing about when our children were small to present day when we could easily fall asleep mid-meditation. Thank you for it all, sis.

Kaushala, a dear friend, how we have laughed, cried and talked together. You have been there discussing this project right from the start, questioning and supporting, taking time to listen. Thank you for all the shared moments whilst our children were growing up, but most of all, thank you for your wonderful, mischievous sense of humour which simply brightens the day.

Lin, thank you for your friendship for the last twenty years, for the gallons of tea and coffee we have drunk together when putting the world to rights, for the Prosecco moments, for your creative input, for the loving care you took with me when taking your amazing photos for the promotion of this book. You are a very talented lady and I am proud to say you are my friend.

Thanks also to my friends, Gari, the man with the wonderful voice, Sue, Dave, Sally, Teresa and Keith, for all the fun and belly aching laughs we have had together.

Thanks to Carol and her colleague, Haidee, for giving me a wonderful makeover for promotional photos, and Jacqueline, the owner of Shellshock, for making it all a wonderful experience.

My thanks go to Michelle who has enthusiastically supported me and made me cry with laughter as we have sorted out the world together.

Special thanks to friends Elio, Christiana and Sabrina for providing me with endless cappuccinos and encouragement when I made the comfy chair in the corner of their delicatessen my second home whilst working on this book.

Thanks to Dave, my brother, Ros and Alan for supporting always and for listening to me endlessly, and to Russell for the fabulous drawing of my guide which was always by my side when I worked.

Thanks to Katie, James, Andrew, Cecilia, Anna, Steve and Judy, you have always shown interest and loving support for everything I have undertaken I am so glad I inherited you all when I married Robert.

I would also like to acknowledge my parents, now in spirit, Hilda and Tom, life was challenging for them but they made me strong, resilient and determined and offered me wisdom I treasure. I know you are close by every day.

To Margery and Billy, now passed but always remembered. You welcomed me into your family and offered caring support whenever needed. I will always be grateful for that.

My thanks also go to my wonderful husband of twenty-five years, Robert, a man who has brought fun, hope, purpose and love into my life. He has supported the family whilst I studied, trained and worked towards my goals, even when he couldn't see where it was all going. Thank you for hanging on in there with me.

Thanks for our two sons, Jamie and Alasdair who make me proud to be their mother. I know sometimes they are not sure how I work, but they support the fact that it is to help people and I truly appreciate that.

I would also like to acknowledge Austin Macauley publishers for enabling me, a first-time author to get the letters out in print and would like to thank all of the staff, the editors and production team for all the hard work they have done to achieve my first book being published.

Thank you all. I am so grateful for all the support you have given me.

Contents

Introduction

50 Letters from Spirit. A Call to Awaken was a gift placed in my care starting in March 2015, but a whole lifetime of events led up to its writing. I cannot say that I directly sat down and planned to write a book, or for that matter decided to work in the field of spiritual guidance and healing. I have had many challenges throughout my life particularly in my teens and early twenties when I experienced great despair with the loss of both my parents after they suffered chronic illnesses. I had been married and divorced and experienced many other forms of loss all before the age of 25. Fortunately, life is not only one type of experience and so I have also had many moments of great joy by starting again in a new marriage, becoming a mother of two children, travelling to exciting new places, having opportunities to learn new skills, learning about spirit and finding my gift.

Looking back now, I can say I am grateful for all of it: the good and the challenging. I cannot say that at the time I relished the challenges, but throughout the winding pathway that is my life, I gradually became aware of what was happening in my life and why. I began to awaken to something more going on.

I had always been interested in the mysteries of the world. I was drawn to Egypt and stories of the Pharaohs, fascinated by those standing stones at Stonehenge and read anything vaguely spiritual. I had been introduced to some ideas of clairvoyance by my mother, who I think had the gift but not the opportunity of learning how to use it fully. My friendships were few when growing up due to moving around the country and changing schools and I often felt isolated and as if I didn't quite fit in. However, I have made some wonderful and genuine friendships with like-minded people in adulthood and together we have explored some of the mysteries of the spiritual world.

I investigated many healing techniques and attended spiritual workshops. I learned from some great teachers in their workshops and seminars, Dr Wayne W Dyer, Esther and Jerry Hicks, Alberto Villodo, Caroline Myss and many more over the years. I read deeper texts on the history of spiritualism authors such as Edgar Cayce, Rudolf Steiner and studied some of the ancient philosophies. A desire to study for a degree, which I had missed out on earlier in life, and through a family member needing some help directed me towards learning with the Open University. I attained a BSc in my forties studying health and social care, psychology of child development, philosophy of mind, thought and experience, world religions, and even death and dying, mainly for grief work. This learning then led me to working with children who learn differently. I had already used complementary and alternative healing methods for my family but came to realise some of these techniques also worked with children who learn differently to the expected norm, and so my interest in these healing therapies grew.

A really bad chest infection which dragged on for weeks led me to Reiki. During a healing session, I had an experience which encouraged me to train in this wonderful healing and I qualified as a Reiki Master. I learned other healing modalities too and went forward helping others. Over the years I studied, learned, worked and experienced all of which brought me to an awareness of self which enabled me to handle the challenges better, quicker and see them for what they really were, lessons and opportunities.

If you like, *I began to understand who I was and why I was here.* I began to awaken to the fact that I was a living spirit in a physical body with a conscious mind working my way through life to experience what I created to evolve my soul. This was a gradual revelation over time but what came next was totally unexpected. It came in September 2013.

Just after my second son had gone off to university, another life change, I felt something was shifting. It wasn't that I was feeling desolate at the fact that both my children were away from home. No, I wasn't desolate, though I obviously missed them. I felt very strongly that we had prepared them as best we could. We had supported them and now it was up to them to take flight and find out who they were. I was excited for them. No, this unsettled feeling, wasn't to do with any of that. I felt the Reiki healing I was doing was coming to a natural end; I felt something was waiting for me, I had no idea what. In fact, as I was to find out, it was 'someone'.

One day in my usual chat to my guides, (I am clairaudient which means that I hear spirit, not physically with my ears though on occasion that can happen, rather hearing in my mind) my main guide took a physical step back; I felt it deep down in the pit of my stomach. Suddenly, I felt very anxious, and he had been there through everything. I felt lost, "Where are you going?" I cried out. "All will be well, others are coming to help." He was still with me as he is my main guide but stepped back to allow me to move forward with other guides and helpers.

So, it began. Over the course of the next few weeks I was introduced to a new guide. I spent time questioning him, making sure he was here for me, inquiring why he had come and what we were to work on together. It was for a different type of healing, through word, to help people find their own strength within themselves. Not a new idea at all, just a forgotten one.

We began to work together delivering one page letters written by hand for the purpose of healing—his energy melding with mine, not quite in full trance or completely automatic writing, but *his words* and *my hand*. The words came thick and fast and seemed to be very straightforward, no nonsense, purposeful, yet delivered with heart and compassion. I challenged us as a team by doing some letters for people who had no real belief in this sort of work and the response was always good.

I had felt this was a practice for a wider audience and so after a while whilst we fine-tuned how we worked together, and knowing there had been mention of a book, I told him I was ready. I was told to be patient by my father, one of my helpers in spirit.

A few days later and honestly getting more frustrated at the lack of information on this book, I respectfully questioned, "Can you give me some idea, a title maybe?"

"There will be letters, 50." Then the headings came very quickly, one after the other, I grabbed pen and paper and wrote them down in order giving each a number. Over the course of 50 days, a number was picked by my guide each day and a letter was handwritten on that subject, so the order of the letters was chosen. He delivered the 50 letters, messages for the people on earth to help them through life, to help them awaken to their own living spirit, handwritten—over 50,000 words.

My guide has offered messages to the world, to humanity, to you, the reader with love from him. He is a kind, considerate soul with an abundance of love, firm but fair, with a mischievous sense of humour and a great compassion for people who need help. Pity is not in his vocabulary, instead he believes in all souls finding their own strength however he believes strongly in love, respect, support and encouragement.

He lived in the Renaissance period in Florence, (1433-1499), and he was a philosopher, theologian, translator, healer and a priest. He was an instigator of many changes, a guide on earth through the period of birth of the arts, sciences, political change and economic development. He wrote letters then to the important and the powerful of the times often urging them to uphold feelings of community, love and respect, to appreciate the beauty in the world to bring about peace in troubled times. (Parallels to what is needed today maybe?) He now writes to offer guidance on many aspects of human ife in the form of letters, again to the important and powerful, to you, the reader, for you are both of these.

The book comes now for we are in a new era of renaissance, rebirth where spiritual awareness is important. It is this period where many people are struggling with change and upheaval, challenge in their lives. It is hoped this book will help you to look a little deeper and awaken to your own spirit within, guiding yourselves forward to a better place even in the most troubled of times.

A Call to Awaken is really looking at your life in a different way, from your soul's point of view. We all have a soul, one that lives every day beneath the personality and mask we offer to the world. The guides ask you to connect with that soul to begin to awaken to the idea that it is soul that is really in the driving seat. To connect with your soul in a way that helps you through the challenges of life because they are not really challenges they are opportunities that your soul has chosen for you to experience in the school of life on earth to enable your soul, the real you, to grow and evolve.

We all go through this process. We are all the same, all religions, all cultures and we are all in this together. All religions, all cultures, all people and their beliefs, all souls are respected by spirit and this author. We just move at a different pace of realisation of our true self. We awaken at different parts of our lives at the point of different experiences, but it is important for humanity as a whole for more of us to awaken to our strengths and our spirit and use our connection to our true spirit in everyday life. It is important in order for us to achieve our purpose, contentment and peace we all strive for in the world. As always, the answer is within.

It begins with you and ends with you. The choice is always yours, in the little things and the bigger things in life. You always have choice and it is this that the guides are trying to awaken in you, that you have choice as a tool to use. The responsibility may be hard to bear for some (see the letter on 'responsibility') but the end result is worth it for it means you can create the life you wish to experience within the soul path you choose. There may be some constraints of agreements you have made, promises if you will, that you made before your soul came to earth, things that you aim to achieve in this life but all in all the choice is yours and once you have made it your guides will support you if it is in your best interests. *Remember there is a difference between what you need and what you want.*

We all have to learn to trust, build a relationship with our own soul and awaken to the power we have within ourselves. Looking outside of ourselves for answers helps a little to find the way through some tough times but the real answers always lie within. You came to earth with a blueprint, all the tools and plans, outlines and decisions you need. There, you already have it all; you just forgot where to look. So now with the help of these messages, maybe just as a starting point it is the hope that you too will start to awaken to your own soul, your own strength, your power to use every day of your life. Through this book of 50 letters, spirit lovingly and respectfully asks you to answer the call to awaken.

Change

Today is yesterday's tomorrow, so change is inevitable. Change stirs up many different emotions for people, it often stirs up negative feelings of worry, fear, even despair, but some relish the excitement of new beginnings beyond the feeling of fear. They feel the rush of the new and excite in the joy of not knowing exactly what is to happen.

We are in control of our own lives and have the tools available to us to create in our lives, just not necessarily the understanding of how we can do this. Perhaps we are not ready to fully realise the tools we have. If we were able to steer our own course (and we can), how would change fit into the plan?

Change comes for many reasons, to prompt us to move forward, to motivate towards something new, to refresh our life patterns, to remove old dusty behaviours which no longer serve us.

So why do we fear change? How fast should change happen? In this new advancing technological world, change is happening fast. (Time of course is relative and not yet fully understood but in the terms of daily life change in technological terms is happening faster each decade.) This has to be so in some realms for new discoveries and even revived ancient ones are coming to move society forward in a new direction.

Change has to happen to enable growth. It is this growth with which we develop our souls. Our perspective changes and so we are able to put our foot forward to a new beginning.

We spoke of steering our own course in life and this is exactly what humanity can do and does but without realising it. The tools we have all been given are choice and free will. Choice to make our own way, choice of thoughts which brings about behaviours, actions and creates the life we are in. It is one of the many universal laws, co-creation, the vital component is faith, faith in your connection to God, to life purpose in serving God through your own physical life. It is a beautiful gift.

Change can be planned and a choice to move forward made, tinged perhaps with anxiety of not knowing the full outcome of your choice. However, this anxiety vs relish of the new is where the excitement of physical life is.

There is something which often goes hand in hand with change, fear. Fear of not being in control, our need to know how our life is going to progress, our need to control ways around the challenges that appear before us.

We expect linear progress through life. We expect change but we often do not welcome and accept it as an old friend which we have seen before, a part of life already lived through which brought us to a new place in life. Instead we struggle and battle against it, fear it and as a result we end up with great challenges and sometimes battles. In order for us to look at our lives differently and make the choice to change, we need to use our own tools which we have been given, one of which is our tool of CHOICE. Choosing a new path, a new small behaviour in our life does not mean giving up control, far from it. It means realising we have complete control over the choices we make and therefore what changes we create in life.

Often making a new choice is feared too. *No choice is better than the wrong choice.* This is a principle many adopt. They fear making the wrong choice, the wrong change so nothing is changed until our souls can bear no more of us treading a path which no longer serves our mission in life. Then change is often forced upon us by our soul working with subconscious mind to bring about situations that will instigate the change required to tread the path our soul came to achieve.

Change is part of the evolution of your soul, and not only is it inevitable, but it should be welcomed. Changes where loss has come about may simply be a clearing out of the old life and a bringing in of the opportunities of the new. Many people have suffered great loss only to go on to create a life they always knew they wanted but it wasn't until the old patterns, old behaviours, old thoughts, old choices had been changed that they could see a new beginning.

Change does not have to be some major overturning of all that you knew and loved. Instead acceptance of *what is*, being consciously aware of *what can be*, and the power of change you possess in your tools given to you by your God can enable small changes of choice which in turn create new patterns in your life.

Sometimes change is full of fear and anxiety but beyond that fear comes a new way forward, a better one, sometimes one beyond your comprehension, a chain reaction of events which lead you to your mission in life, a change that develops your learning as a spiritual entity in a physical body. In this way our souls evolve and change becomes a useful tool in our everyday lives.

Welcome change, embrace change, accept change and look forward to the results. The changes that happen today reflect on tomorrow and so beyond but we always have choice to continually change and grow and evolve, to change our life plan. We steer the course with the divine tools our God gave us.

The God you follow guides and supports you in your choices and changes in your life under your own free will, your God loves you unconditionally to have given you these wonderful tools of choice and free will to enable you to grow.

Living the full embodied experience of physical life, being a full expression of who you are is the goal here on earth. Change is an inevitable part of this, because none of us stand still, we are all different today from who we were yesterday for we have experienced a little more of life each day lived.

Change is nothing to be feared. It is an exciting tool to the new experiences you wish to have, some may seem negative at the time, but they are all lessons for your soul and by using your tool of choice, free will, you can steer towards a positive outcome which will give you great wisdom, faith in your abilities and in your life as a (divine entity) living a physical life evolving your soul. Without change, there is limitation.

Tomorrow brings a new challenge of change but it is a new beginning, a new choice, a change towards a new you, a more consciously aware you, steering yourself through your life with courage to make new choices and face change. Change is there as part of growth and is to be embraced not feared. See change as an exciting gift, a tool to bring new energy into your life and all will be well.

Relationships

We have many relationships throughout our physical lives. We have parents, enemies, acquaintances, loved ones, wives, husbands and our children. These are complex and wonderful treasures full of learning and experiences; however, the most important relationship we seem to overlook is the one with ourselves. We give very little attention on an everyday basis to who we are in relationship with our true being, with our soul; our emotional-self reacts, interacts and experiences many emotions through the relationships we choose in life. Many relationships may be difficult and complicated a game of to and fro, point scoring, even fear based relationships where control is the important factor instead of love and the growth of respect.

A relationship between souls seems to evaporate into a chasm of materialism and what one can get from another. To see the real soul of the one before you is not considered, it is important to see the real person without judgement. This may seem difficult or not even on the agenda but if you make a step in that direction you will begin to understand yourself more and so begin to experience the real self. We are all souls in physical bodies learning lessons and our relationships are part of that learning about ourselves and others. These relationships offer experiences where you can offer support yet not decide for them, laugh and cry with them and decide when to love and let go of them.

Deep experience or growth of soul is derived from interactions in our relationships with others on earth. They enable us to learn who we really are and develop personality traits where we can see where our strengths and weaknesses are. To see who we are and who we are not. Your soul would find it hard to express its true being without others in your life and so find it difficult to follow its path and what it has come to achieve.

We choose the family we share our physical lives with. Agreements are made at soul level for all those learnings and experiences you will mutually have. There is learning in all, the good, the bad, the ugly as you say. Relationships need a foundation and that foundation needs to be the realisation of who we truly are. Once you operate from your true being, your relationships will be on a new level, one where you attract the frequency of honesty, of love without conditions, one of respect for the true being you are, regardless of the façade of personality we believe we have to offer to the world. We are talking about deep and true knowing of self, of the uniqueness of self, of the true being and purpose you have brought to the world. In knowing this self, this relationship of knowing yourself, you can truly connect with people on an authentic level bringing them a piece of your true being, revealing a condition of allowing and accepting which in turn allows them to be themselves. No judgement, just being. This part of divine self then enables a true connection to those you hold dear in this world and opens up enormous possibilities to connect with humanity to bring about a connection, a world connection, a respect of diversity without abuse, judgement and criticism, instead building a world of respect, peace, love, support, community.

This brings huge rewards for individual souls but also great learning for humanity itself. For all souls are connected in the physical life on earth.

Earth is a place of soul learning, growth and evolution. Our relationship with our self is the foundation for the way forward in an ever changing world. We can become more self-aware and then more consciously aware. There is an era of becoming more consciously aware of self and just how we can operate and create our own reality with a connection to Source, Creator, God whichever term you prefer.

Many teachers who have trodden the earth before this generation have declared that change starts with self. So, create thoughts which allow positive change, and choose thoughts which enable self to move forward positively without limitation. The work always begins with our relationship with self. We cannot truly believe that what we feel is missing in ourselves can be supplied by someone else. We must find the courage to seek within ourselves and so explore where we can work on the things we are to learn instead of holding others to count, or blame them for not providing us with what we need.

It is time for a new Renaissance. This era (the original Renaissance) was one where the emotional soul was released to humanity through the beauty of music, art and a respect of culture. The soul begged to express and begged to be heard against a backdrop of political control and power and many atrocities in the name of religion. When you behold art from this era, the subject matter may be austere but the beauty of the figures, the richness of colour and exuberance of the artists enables the soul to find the beauty within, which it sought to express and bring to the world a new appreciation of humanity and what it could achieve. It offered a consoling warmth of spirit, an uplifting along with music of the era as an alternative to the harsh religious and political boundaries being fought over. It revealed a softer side to humanity, a prelude to an historic cultural revolution of artistic expression.

In the same way today, we have many harsh realities in life, political, religious and environmental. Yet there is a new era of becoming consciously aware of what human beings can be, are, and always have been, a combination of spirit and physical. This era is for a dawning of how the two work together consciously to create a better world, a world where souls can truly express the beauty of their uniqueness without judgement.

It is time for this new Renaissance where our souls must burst forth with the truth we hold in our hearts, expressing the richness in community, the love of the earth despite the backdrop of materialism and desire for more things.

Seek the beauty of a true relationship where you are who you are, a unique being, bring to the world your gifts and express your loves, passions, offer them in service and receive service from others, developing a community of cooperation instead of competition.

This new renaissance means a shift in direction, a rising of frequency, a belief in a more authentic lifestyle but it has a cost. The cost is personal responsibility.

People often say that we didn't choose to come into this world. This is not so, you did just that, and for a reason. Your soul chose with purpose to become more consciously aware within your physical life. Previous lifetimes of the centuries that have gone before have seen a gradual evolution of what mankind can do. It has not all been without its unwelcome outcomes but generally mankind has moved forward intellectually and technologically yet spiritual connection which was present and dominant when life was simpler in the other two realms has meant that our spiritual connection has faded.

This new era demands rejuvenation and a surge forward in spiritual thinking to match the scientific, intellectual and technological progression of mankind. It has to play catch-up and then move beyond. It has to offer a connection between all these facets of mankind. It invites mankind to become spiritually and consciously aware of whom human beings truly are and match this with physical life and all its progression. In other words, to claim humanity's spirit as being from God and to use the power of thought, choice and free will consciously positively in combination with its physical developments for the benefit of the world.

This is a new way forward but it is always your choice. Always. So the beginning is choosing to have a true relationship with who you really are and bring this to your many relationships you hold dear. Seek and reveal your true self. Offer your true being in service to humanity through all your relationships throughout your life. Embrace who you are and enjoy a renaissance (a rebirth) of your own.

Relationships are an important part of who you are but to truly achieve your purpose you must bring who you truly are to that relationship. Then build on this solid foundation and watch as your relationships develop into a rich and deep cooperative and supportive treasure which leads to a new understanding of each other, allowing and accepting each other as you truly are with all the gifts from God that you all possess as individual unique reflections of humanity with loving divine souls. Let the treasure of being who you truly are lead you to a new beginning and a far richer deeper experience in the physical world.

Grief

Grief follows loss and is a difficult string of emotions to contend with as a human being. Loss can be of a person close to you, family, a friend, a job, a lifestyle, possessions, and even an expectation. There are many facets to grief, but in the Victorian era, death was a prominent part of life and so many rituals surrounding loss evolved and long periods of mourning and stages of grief expected. Many approaches to death and loss in general are still linked with this very outward expression of mourning. Psychology expresses several stages of grief and mourning, listing various emotions usually gone through as part of this grieving mechanism.

One of the most common emotions recognised as part of the grief process is anger; this emotion in itself is multi-faceted. It is a complex emotion we as human beings are taught to supress and so as part of grief, although a perfectly natural emotion often prolongs the feeling of grief because it is a part of our emotions we are taught less about and not directed on how we could manage as a part of our normal education. In addition many fear loss and particularly a death as we are not taught to discuss this openly as part of life and so in many cultures it becomes a shocking and extremely hard to deal with event in our lives.

Many other emotions accompany this feeling of grief, denial, regret, detachment, lethargy and many more. Every person grieving is different. Different situations leave us with different degrees of feelings of loss and grief. There is a positive, however, even to loss and grief and with great respect let me explain. Firstly, grief and its many stages should be seen as very natural. It is an expression of the love you have shared in your life. The deep and sometimes overwhelming feeling that comes with loss means that you have certainly loved and loved deeply. It is the reverse side of the coin to the deep connection you have felt for the person you have lost. The feeling of loss in a way celebrates the connection. Hand-in-hand with the feeling of desolation and the natural negative feeling of loss and grief is also the wonderful love you held. This realisation may come at a much later stage of grief but it is one to be considered.

In this love there can be a celebration of the unique life that was present in the world, an uplifting feeling of the shared life, the family and experiences which you are grateful for. Nothing is permanent, all things change, we are just travelling through this physical life.

Any connections we make on a love level are for the joy of life and we are here to be joyful and live a fulfilled life.

When a soul decides it is time to leave the physical world and return to the spiritual home, it has in essence decided it has completed its mission in this lifetime. It is the choice of the soul to leave, always. This leaving of the physical world is feared because we forget our spiritual home when we join the physical world and often this fear is not discussed. This makes the grief stages harder for those left behind. Why now? It is important to remember that life is a celebration and returning to spirit is a celebration of life as well.

Part of the hurt of grief comes from a misunderstanding from the life you live. The challenges and hardships are for learning and growth. Suffering need not be, even in these hard times. Suffering comes from denial and a battle and resistance against the inevitable. With acceptance there is a peace. Grief is natural, but it is a stage of life and needs to be worked through accepted and moved along to transform into something new.

There are cases where people have "lost everything" and received donations and help and suddenly realised people care. They begin to see not so many 'things' are needed; they appreciate kindness, the community, the cosseting in love, and their perspective changes.

Families may grieve in a different way for the difficulties their children are born with, perhaps they grieve the expectation of a perfectly healthy child. Often they experience a deep and rewarding relationship with that child who teaches them a different point of view and a different capability of perfect love.

Those people who have lost a particular loss of a lifestyle perhaps due to loss of limbs fighting to protect a cause or people they hold dear may find a way forward. They may mourn the loss of one lifestyle but find courage and strength they did not know they had. They go forward campaigning for those who cannot or achieve awards in a new sport and achieve great things in realms they otherwise would not have found.

Many losses are hard to bear. They leave deep scars and some feel like they will never be healed. It is time to celebrate what *you have now,* what *you had* and what *you will have.* All of these things will be different because you never remain the same. Your emotions evolve as does your body. Your body, your mind, your spirit and your soul are all connected. The combination is the complete and unique you. So, everyone experiences grief differently and it is an experience we all have at some time in our life.

If you avoid feeling the emotions of grief, working your way through it to the other side then it will pop up when you expect it least and maybe in different form. Maybe just the anger will be released, maybe in a new way over something small but it may be part of supressed emotion not dealt with. It is important to deal with your grief with respect knowing it is natural, feeling it fully, then moving it forward and letting the pain go leaving the celebration of the life lived and loved. Grief is a powerful set of emotions which are to be respected. Discuss it, accept it, and move at your own pace in a truthful manner. Then gradually see the positives you had and have and will have. Look to the present and build on it. Never forget, always be thankful. Live your life now so regrets are few later and above all love the life you have; it is precious.

Experience fully the moments and the people you have today and love the opportunities, bless the mess, accept and see the challenges as a way forward and evolve your soul to its limit.

Enjoy all of life, raise up your energy, your frequency and the pain of loss and grief in time will fall away into the place it rightly belongs, as an experience, learning, but not a place to stay forever for that limits what else is waiting in your life. In staying in grief there is no celebration of life that was, is and will be.

The Buddhist way believes there is suffering because we want and attach to things and people. They profess a life of non-attachment. This non-attachment does not mean one of not caring or even one of not connecting. For connecting to your fellow man is of paramount importance to your growth.

Non-attachment is connected more to do with letting things be as they are and appreciating without wanting to possess and allowing things to go when it is time. This loving, appreciating without possessing has benefit. People change, evolve, come and go, they are loved and sadly their physical being is lost. They are always here. Spirit survives and the connection is always here through your heart.

Grief and the deep sense of loss, the physical loss of someone dear to us often closes the very centre that we need to keep open to continue the spiritual connection to that soul, our heart. Grief is a hard experience to go through as a human being. Yet like all things it can be transmuted. It must be felt and dealt with, with respect and understanding but we must also choose life again afterwards. Grief is a part of life we do not wish upon ourselves but it is an unavoidable one if we have loved and to love is divine. To love is human and we must not stop being that, loving humans.

Relationship with God

We are all connected, this is so whether we follow a particular religion or not. Religion in itself is a method of connection. We consider religions or having no religion as equal. They are all pathways, but what is really important is the relationship they bring about. The relationship they connect you to, the opening of a channel between you and your relationship with God. It is the everyday dialogue and relationship you have with your God and how that brings your divine self within you to your life and those who are important in your lives.

Your connection to your God, your dialogue with God on a daily basis is extremely important, for it is this connection which reminds your soul of the purpose of its service here on earth.

The practise of doctrine of a particular religion is not what is referred to here—though this may be of great help to some to reach the level of connection with God. It is humbly requested that people do not get too tangled with the doctrine of a particular religion, by all means practise it if it serves you in the provision of a path to a true connection on a personal level with your God. You are all worthy of this connection, and it cannot be otherwise as you are of God, from God, in the service of God. The important focus is on your personal relationship with God and how this can be brought to your lives.

In all religions God represents unconditional love. It may take different forms and offer different rules and regulations within different religions but ultimately it is God, the parent with unconditional love for all souls upon the earth. That is a beautiful concept. So your personal relationship, your two way dialogue, in your own language, in your own way is always one of choice, one of perfection in that moment.

Offering prayers of gratitude and thanks, asking for guidance, offering your service to help others in the world are part of this two way personal dialogue. Spreading the love of God in a different way from a foundation of a personal relationship built on mutual respect and love and not fears.

This may mean that those belonging to the same faith interpret their personal relationship with God differently to another person of same faith but the intention that is held in love to help fellow man need not be the same as your neighbour, for we are all unique.

Fear, punishment, destruction, judgement are not based in love and particularly not divine love. The interpretation of ideas of religion is left open to choice.

If your interpretation leads to a destructive act then this is not resonating with the high frequency of love of God. Bringing your frequency to a personal relationship with your God can only raise your energy and you will live your life on a higher frequency without the low energy of fear and the actions which come about through fear as opposed to love.

Individual choice and free will has consequence. Community, group choice collectively following the route of love, born out of a truthful loving relationship with your God can and will make a difference on earth. What community, society, groups of loving humans choose to accept will make a difference to the energy of the reality constructed in physical life. In other words what you choose as an individual as a loving value for society and if this is agreed as a group at that same energy level of love then it will impact on real life if enough agree on that level. This begins with your relationship with God and so raising your own energy level and acting on that frequency in an intention of love, not on a pious and intellectual level, this relationship has positive influence as a ripple effect within communities and this then has influence on behaviours.

A group of individuals may agree on soul level to follow the same loving route with a respect for diversity, uniqueness and a will to express your relationship with God through your own unique individual life because of a mutual wish within the society they share. Peace on earth can be achieved by a shift in appreciating diverse and wonderful cultures and by remembering and learning from the past. Fear can provoke conflict. Conflict is derived from separation, separation from a personal relationship with God and separation from the knowledge of who we really are in terms of our spiritual being and connection to all and to God.

To resolve conflict, we as individual souls need to be aware of who we are and of our divine connection. Whichever God you worship and whichever religion you are part of or even if you have no particular religious faith, your belief in yourself as an individual soul and the capabilities of that soul in service in community and in living in cooperation and faith within this community is indeed what can achieve resolution.

We all have passions and passion put forward for the community of humanity, use of gifts for service can only bring about a deepening of the relationship your soul has with your God. It is a dialogue between the individual and their God which in this era will aid the unification of diverse cultures. It is a slight shift within set religions to put responsibility on individual souls rather than the doctrine of that whole religion. This slight change will then unify the whole religion in a different synergy and in turn help unite the different cultures and religions within those cultures.

Service not for service's sake of how it looks but service for your passion's sake and this in turn results in evolution of individual souls and humanity as a whole.

Enhancing your personal relationship with God enables you to feel supported through challenge; there is always support for you. Not deciding for you, for only you have that gift, the gift of choice and free will but supporting in a loving way.

Actions born out of fear, aggression, destruction, judgement, operate on a low frequency. We are all made up of energy and operate on different frequencies during our life dependent upon where we are in a particular situation. We can raise our energy up or lower it. It is our choice.

Of course, God is operating on the highest frequency of unconditional love and will not support actions on a lower frequency intent on harm. An individual has free will to ask for help, and once this is asked for, God will support to raise individual frequency but it is our choice to ask for help when we are in despair to be raised to a level of hope. This is where prayer enters into dialogue with God.

We are entering an era of the new Renaissance, re-birth. It is an era where technology and the physical world's new and wonderful inventions will move forward but there is something which will go hand-in-hand with this. It is a meeting of the spiritual and the physical. It is a quest for the physical body to become aware of its spiritual foundation and be consciously aware of the power of thought, of the spoken word and its action. To raise our energy the personal relationship with our Source, God or Creator, whichever word you prefer is an element of great importance, so from our endeavour to have a personal relationship with God this will lead to an understanding of our spiritual self-connected to God, our uniqueness, our gifts and tools we can raise our individual energy in our own lives and choose wisely, choose to follow who we are, fulfil the purpose for which we were put on this earth.

Inspiring others to find in their uniqueness their own dialogue with a higher frequency, God in whichever religion or even no religion is important, to encourage this personal interaction on a spiritual level.

In rising to our best as we are all connected in spirit, we raise all, we connect with higher energy, higher values and live by our own individual high energies through communing with God and placing that in the physical world enabling a more loving respectful diverse society.

Focus upon the individual relationship; focus on that and other things will slowly fall into place. Joyful and peaceful respectful community can be born out of individual relationships with God using doctrine of religion not as the focal point but instead as a helpful tool to raise energy. Remember religion is a practise of loving a God that loves you unconditionally. Connection to that can be in a unique way but always within a high energy of love, mutual respect and without control, power or judgement. It is time in this era of new renaissance to bring back the love into our relationship with God and consequently with humanity.

Love

Love is the most precious treasure. It is the reason for life, expressed in life on earth. There is only one way to achieve our ultimate goal set by the soul. There is really only one motivation for all things that we strive for upon earth. We act in the name of love, we search for love, and we regret and feel we have something missing in the name of love. We feel certain negative feelings follow certain behaviours through an apparent lack of love. It is the key emotion to our triumphs and our troubles. So how do we really define this feeling of love? We have to hold this as a connection to our heart from Source. It originates in our souls from our Source, Creator, God. We are nurtured and loved in our formative years of life or we have a lack of love in these years. Both situations, though, can lead to a realisation to real love and our ability to feel it and pass it on through our lives.

Let us, those in the world of spirit, explain. A lack of love can bring the soul to search and look for it in many places perhaps at first not really knowing what is missing. Then maybe a life of hardships, challenges and wrong choices may ensue. However, through it all one can begin to see patterns that do not serve the soul and so learning begins. From this an exploration can start and a discovery of the strength of self, perhaps a reconnection to Source, God, Creator. A realisation that true love comes from within the individual, firstly given by Source to the soul. It's then for the soul to search and find self-worth, self-esteem and self-love. Self-love is a term which often gets confused with selfishness. Self-love is not selfish. It is of paramount importance as it can only be that an individual can give what it has. We need a root foundation, born in love and knowledge of who we are spiritually, emotionally, intellectually and physically combined together so we can love fully and truly. Often we place conditions upon self as well. I am not worthy of love because I am not like this or that. I am different from the crowd. Well, we are all different. That is an important part of who you are.

So we are on a journey of finding out that we are worthy of love and that above all we have to give that to ourselves, to make a strong foundation to offer our gifts in the form of our physical life to the world. In our relationships with others, in our way we serve in life.

Another scenario may be that we do have great love at the start of our lives and having had that experience find it hard to find in other relationships. Once again an exploration begins, judgements are made, targets of perfection are sought and missed and disappointment fills hearts and relationships.

Once again a realisation eventually that the journey to true love starts with self, loving self in the same way Source offered to you in the beginning means that when you truly love yourself warts and all, it means you carry yourself in value and respect and so attract to you other people that also love you in that way with the respect and value you hold for yourself without arrogance and over confidence but in peace and contentment that you know your own worth in love. This then is a good foundation for you to love, respect and value another soul.

When this is in place it is a small step to enable others to see their value in themselves, to be able to pass this on.

Love is multi-faceted and offered in many ways in many different relationships and forms. Happiness comes from the love of God flowing through your soul and your awareness of that love in your physical life, having that reassurance that even when you are alone you are always loved. You are always connected to love from God, Source, Creator. It is this reassurance which enables us to remember our own self-worth, remind ourselves to love ourselves enough to give ourselves what we need and then go on to become who we truly are, a magnificent expression of God in an individual soul living in a physical body.

Life without love is impossible, for the love of our God, never leaves us. It is US that separates us from the possibility of love by thinking that we are not worthy of God's love, love of our family or friends. In this feeling of being apart from love we make choices which do not work for us and then follow a path which confirms our lack of self-worth and lack of self-love.

To correct this we need to reconnect with self, reconnect with the heart centre, ask for help from Source to show us and help us re-establish our own worth. Then on this foundation grasp the opportunity of help that is put our way. We need to make ourselves strong and offer ourselves the respect and love we deserve. It is an important part of life on earth. Self-love is the source of true unconditional love because we are part of God, our self that is soul is part of God and so cannot be anything other than love. For when we have that loving reassurance we seek to offer that to others, not to be a crutch, yet to support, not to do for, yet to show how to do, not to expect, yet to allow attainment.

There are subtle differences to true love; it is an accepting of self and an allowing of others their own self-acceptance.

When we recognise the true feeling of self-love then it is easy to support the expectations of others, enable them to give to themselves what they are worth.

This is not a way to make the world self-centred, quite the contrary it means that there is cooperation rather than competition, there is no need to be a certain way to receive acceptance, diversity, uniqueness is recognised. It is normal to be different, and there is no normal, but there is beauty, diversity, connectedness, self-worth and above all, there is love. It is the sweetest thing; it is the essence of life.

Joy/Pleasure

Pure pleasure is hard to come by in this modern world. It is sought in many ways, in love, in work, in peace, sometimes in negative ways for the body in alcohol and drugs.

Pure pleasure is really another way of saying peace, contentment. Happy with your life, contentment in what you really have is all to do with what is inside of yourself. Once joy and contentment is on the inside, the simple things in life start to give pure pleasure and joy.

Often seeking for a feeling of joy that is bigger than us, we look for an overwhelming burst of joy, which can happen and is wonderful when it does, but often pure pleasure, contentment is in a feeling of sameness, level and peaceful, high energy levelled.

How do we find joy, peace, contentment in everyday life when worries barge in? Worries about family, health, money, friends, work, partners... how can all this be overcome to achieve joy every day? Simply by reconnecting to Source, to your knowing that all will be well in the end and that life has its way, and there are lessons here to be learned. They seem hard lessons my friends and sometimes you feel devastated but they are lessons your soul has chosen. So please bear with the challenges and feelings you have which are far from joy. These feelings will pass and courage to feel the joy of life rises again.

It sometimes feels there is no way out but you know you are always supported by the love of Source, God, or Creator (whichever title you prefer). You are part of His creation and as such were made to experience joy in life. Love from Source will always be present for you. Guides, angels and the love of God will steer you from the feeling of despair (if you ask for help for free will and choice cannot be interfered with so help has to be requested) and bring you to a new level of appreciation of joy. The joy in things you already have but perhaps did not see before.

Joy and peace are really a choice, a choice of thoughts. Something you have available to you always. It is a choice about everything that you have, a courageous choice to feel the best you can about a given situation. A choice not to be brought down by the sadness you feel at the challenge before you. Life is duality. It is the hardships and the love.

When you are amidst desolation it is important to see that all of this is the soul's choice. Your soul has chosen this life, its lessons and its joys. You have free will and choice as your tools throughout your life and so my friends it is for you to implement these tools in order to receive the full benefits of the duality of the challenges you have chosen.

Perhaps it is hard to believe that you would choose some of the hardships but acceptance of this brings with it a realisation that your soul is in control and has your best interests always at heart. When you come to this earth you are born into your body with your soul purpose.* When you leave this earth, the physical body is no longer needed but the soul returns to the plane where higher-self resides.

What has the soul achieved in this time?

It has experienced care, support, innocence, disaster, loss, love, joy, peace, war, exhilaration, jealousy, poverty, wealth, health, abundance and so much more.

It has interacted with other souls. It has been supported and it has been ill. It has been well. It has experienced, learned and loved. That is the gift the soul carries. It never loses all it has learned. It carries it from previous lives; it carries it now and into the future.

The peace and contentment, pleasure /joy you seek is in your own soul, and in the knowledge that your soul, who you really are, is eternal, that your soul is growing with every experience you have on earth.

All life has learning, all life has growth, all life can be joyful and all life has the ability to add value and to carry this joy of learning and growth forward. It is for you to carry in your heart the joy of this experience. This is where the real contentment is, the contentment of coming through challenge and still have the joy of your soul in your heart.

We are not suggesting that we just wave a magic wand and all will be well. We are suggesting that a deep knowing of who you really are, a spiritual soul in a

---

* N.B. throughout the book my guide refers to sole purpose and soul purpose. Sole purpose he regards as the single purpose, the main purpose we are here which is growth and evolution of the soul.

When he is referring to soul purpose he means purpose of individual soul or souls which may be one goal of learning or many lessons depending on individual choices made.

physical body will enable an awareness, a remembering of why we are here and so bring a different perspective to the challenges of the day. These walls, these obstacles before us may just be doors to open and awareness of self is the key.

We have all lived many lives some with more joy than others. This was our choice before we came to earth but once here we have choices of how to deal with what we have put before ourselves. How will we treat the challenge and enable growth within the life we have chosen?

It is time to acknowledge we get embedded too much in the "realities" of the challenge on earth. We forget our spiritual connection and the meaning for the lives we live. This spiritual remembrance is where our joy is seated for the peace and contentment comes in feeling re-united with that part of us we felt was missing but was with us all the time, our spiritual self, our soul, our connection to Source. In this knowledge, in this revelation, that we are already all we were meant to be but just simply forgot that side of ourselves, in this, comes overwhelming peaceful joy.

We are all in the same process of evolution of the soul, yet we are all unique in the way we tackle our growth and learning. So within the hustle and bustle of the troubles of life, seek out the joy within yourself, seek the contentment, do what makes you happy, do what you have passion for whether you feel it will succeed or not and as you go bless the mess, encourage love, enable growth. Be aware of the trouble yet not attached to it. Allow resolution, forgive, let go of the unworthy feelings, respect your soul, be who you are and allow others the same, offer and receive support and compassion.

In all of this is contentment and in that peace there is joy, pleasure and meaning in life.

Tremendous learning brings about magnificent living, great joy and love in all you do, passion for your interests, discovering you, being connected. Oh there is so much joy in this. Allow this in everything you do, interactions with friends, with family, with activities and learning.

There are times which are hard and these come to remind us of who we are, why we are here and how we have the power to turn things around, to stop seeing the obstacle but instead find the key to open the door and move forward.

Good times and bad, appreciate both, for they bring learning, growth, be thankful, be grateful but above all else be joyful.

Thought and Its Power

Thought indeed has great power and we need to understand and address how this great power really works. There is a great deal of wonder that we do not have control over our thoughts. Indeed it appears too complex for humans to consider, that the power they hold in their thoughts is immense and one that can change their lives and can just as well constrict their lives in this moment of time.

They cannot believe trails of words, wonderings; negative and positive inner dialogue can actually help or hinder and create what actually happens in the physical world.

So how does it work? It is a simple recipe, a combination of discipline of thought and creative imagination and a large sprinkle of faith, (which is where humanity often goes astray).

We live in an ever increasing world of science and technology and the world of spiritual things is often left unnoticed, a thing that existed before true science was discovered, or perhaps we should say uncovered.

In fact, the reverse is true. In ancient times of alchemy, there was an intended melding of science and spiritual matters. New methods in medicine evolved though crude at first but great technologies were reached and sadly at one time abused but before this there was spiritual awareness: awareness of the soul, human spirit and the creative power it held.

Even today individual souls create marvellous things not even contemplated 20 years ago. Advancement in technology however emphasises the need for spiritual re-discovery. We are not talking about religion here though by your own choice that may be one path but in conjunction with religion, technology and science, a third path may be required.

It is the power of knowing and with this the power of thought. Thought you may perceive as our minds at work and it is true our minds are the conduit but thoughts are things, they are energy being transferred. We have full control of the thoughts we choose. If we think one thing about ourselves with conviction what will come to us are situations which enforce that thought, for our thoughts are there, for creation. If we deviate from the path of creation in a positive way to something more negative, filling our thoughts, choosing our thoughts with negative inner dialogue then we create a life before us filled with emphasis on this negative dialogue. If, however, we focus on a positive result with faith and conviction that we can create the positive outcome, focussing upon strengths to achieve it, skills we have with a willingness to believe it is possible, a deep faith it will happen, then by the laws of the universe it cannot be any other way.

We concentrate too much on: what is not working, what is negative and what is going wrong. We focus on all the reasons why we cannot do something, and why we can't be who we are.

We do not realise we are already the full person who we are meant to be, and it is all within us. We have just forgotten we already have all the skills we need to put our dreams in place.

We need to focus, choose the best thoughts for the purpose in hand and believe in the power of thought. Then to add to the faith and conviction you have, put some extra energy by acting in the right direction.

It is creation at its best. It is your creation; it is your choice. Of course, the universe will not support ill will, and so although you may choose this then some negativity will come your way if you choose this for others. That is law.

So we have choice, of the hundreds and thousands of words and dialogue that goes through the brain every day. What then if we start creating a new world for ourselves aligned with our sole purpose. This then would have a ripple effect on those around you. Then they begin to learn and understand how to do this through their thought, then they pass it on and soon we have a much disciplined group learning how to manage their thoughts with creative power.

Allowing and accepting this power is the hardest part for it means that you as humans have to acknowledge your own greatness, your own divine power.

Many are already using this creativity for new ideas in medicine, communications and many other areas. They are seeing their ideas form in the physical world to bring about change, growth and evolution.

Soon people in this era of the new Renaissance will create a way of living, housing, energy, providing food and water where it is needed without destroying the beauty of the earth.

It is but a thought away, with the connection to God, Creator, or Source (as you prefer) through religious faith if you so choose, not so much through doctrine but by the power of direct and individual connection to God, by invention and science and technology and by the acceptance of the power of creation each human being has.

You have before you in this era of Renaissance, a destiny on earth full of marvellous creation.

A creation with cooperation, learning from each other, a time where providing security, care and compassion for all those who need it. This IS easily attainable.

It is time for a rebirth where humanity can choose its own creations by now being aware of what has already been happening for centuries but without realisation that reality, a new reality, is only a thought away.

Thought, choice and free will are humanity's gifts and they are ones to be treasured, acknowledged and finally used with the end creation aligning to individual sole purpose, creating a better life for individuals and humanity alike. What a thought... your thought?

Earth

We need to care for the place where we live. The earth is a precious gift. It has the ability to look after itself despite the way that humanity has treated her in places. It has the great ability to heal despite the pollution and the over use of its natural minerals. It is a balancing act. The earth provides environments to sustain an inordinate variety of animals in order to uphold a wonderful eco-system to provide for and sustain all humanity and all life upon the earth. However, humanity is not re-cognising the need for balance and instead is trying to reap as much reward from the provision of minerals on the earth without replacing enough.

Animals have become extinct and there is great sadness over this when an animal species dies out due to poaching and through habitats being destroyed.

We are not asking for humanity to go backwards living by campfires in small houses. We are asking that new technologies move forward and new consideration be given to the benefits the earth gives and therefore the replenishing which has to take place as a two-way contract and respect for the earth on which you live and thrive.

Natural balance is important to health and well-being of all creatures. Particularly as the frequency, the energy of the earth can be felt in our own energy bodies, then in turn within our physical bodies.

If we do not learn to look after the earth then eventually the earth will cleanse itself.

There will be storms, earthquakes and natural movements to refresh that which is polluted.

She needs to know she is loved, that she is respected for that which she provides and so she needs to be aware that she is cared for. Mother Earth brings forth such beauty, we only really see what we have or had when things change or move on.

The earth is a living thing all energy generation can be natural; there are simple sources which have not really been explored yet. The waves, solar and wind power are all good ways to provide energy but there are minerals which will provide individual energy sources within individual homes and this is a long lasting source which may need to be renewed only once in every 90 years. This source provides without harm. So we can live in a new world, a forward technology without damaging what is around us and without hurting our environment. A crystal which can sit inside a unit and provide a way to drive a generator of sorts which provides heat and light. It will be an inexpensive source and one which can be used anywhere in the world. It is deep blue like the sea and like a sapphire.

Scientists have already been thinking like this and soon it will be tested. They are unsure which minerals and how to encapsulate this energy inexpensively and with least disturbance to the earth. There are sources under the sea, also in mountains where it is cold but all must be mined with great care and balance, no explosions. This is one big source of energy and other natural energy can complement. It is about working in balance with the earth with cooperation and consideration.

Rain forests need to be protected and new ways of finding and earning a living in these areas need to be found. Destroying what is there is a short-term plan and really brings no lasting benefit to any in the area. The damage will have repercussions with the climate for many years to come and so for the peoples of that area.

Without consideration to this earth and all her gifts we will not thrive in a way humanity could. We will end up with great costs, particularly with our health and well-being.

Our environment in our homes can make us well or it can make us sick. It is the same on a larger scale for the whole of humanity and the earth.

The balance in the water is important too, the way we fish to provide food and the way we treat larger animals is important to the eco-system.

The dolphins and the whales have great wisdom of the eco-system of the sea. They provide a way of keeping specific plankton and other less known energies within the food chain and help to keep the balance; they are healers of the sea.

Dolphins communicate with humans and befriend them in a way to connect humans to the joy of the sea in order to encourage respect for their home. They are creatures of love and wisdom. Tuna nets are their enemy but we are trying to address this. They are serene and clever animals and they tune into the energy of humanity. They have the ability to heal by pitch and frequency, balancing human energies. That is why swimming with dolphins brings about a rewarding experience, particularly for children with a high energy who have learning differences because of an imbalance within their own energy frequency. They can tune in on this different dimension and connect on a different level with the child rebalancing and healing.

There are wonderful things unfound in the sacred areas on the earth. The knowledge of these things to some extent is protected by the holy men, though even they are unaware of all that is there, and this is as it should be for the world has to be aware of the choices they make in order for these further gifts to be revealed.

It is a matter of keeping balance, and so until man can truly understand the balance between his spiritual energy and his physical energy, he cannot really understand how the gifts of energy work and how to achieve the balance between earth and man. More work is to be done on this.

There are mysteries of the earth that will unfold when the time is correct and man is ready to receive them. We ask that first you become aware of how you are in the big picture and who you really are, your gifts and your energy and then to concentrate on how to move into balance with the earth and all its secrets.

Blessings for the earth are sent always, for the earth itself and its wonderful people. Please be kind to the earth and to the people as well. It is for the benefit of all in this era of new renaissance and for the generations to come following this rebirth.

Silence

In the silence there is much to hear, the beating of your own heart, the root of your soul and of your physical being. In this busy world time needs to be taken to listen to your own heartbeat, the rhythm of your soul.

How do you want to work with your soul in this world? Whose rhythm are you following? Is it your own heartbeat? Is it your own passion?

When we are focussing on our own lives, our busy lives with family, work, travel, friends, food, drink, hobbies, ambitions, relationship, social media... do we take time to stop and breathe in the silence?

The technological age is welcomed but there has to be balance. There must be time to stop and listen to the beauty of the soul. To stop, review and focus on the important, you must throw out the unimportant. Thoughts in the silence can be used to redirect and change the pattern of your life. It is only when you stop and BE, that silence becomes a vessel to peace and contentment. There is no need to do a particular action. The Doing is in being; the action is a change of thought followed by imagining the positive outcome and conviction that it will be delivered, in faith, no doubt.

That is what true faith is referred to in many scriptures, faith in a better outcome.

Silence is a gift to yourself to give you time to review, to BE with your heart, to be with your soul. To re-connect with whom you truly are, to combine your spirit with your physical body, to continue to work from your soul and move forward in your physical life from the perspective of your soul, living from your soul.

There has been much value of silence in the practice of meditation and yoga by many spiritual masters. Using the breathing techniques to quieten the body and enable an easier commune with God. These all have great value. We however urge you to not be deterred by such techniques and instead simply have the intention and practice of including a few minutes silence in your day, to use this space to bless your lives, for thanks and gratitude. To take one deep breath to inhale the wisdom of your soul and expel the unwanted clutter of life. Just sit in a park, a garden, in the summer sunshine, to breathe and BE.

In that moment bless the mess, the troubles in life, be thankful and grateful for the good in your life, ask, claim, focus and visualise, imagine what positive change you want to make. Then see it in fruition. Allow it, accept it, receive it, how does it look, how does it feel, know it. Feel how it feels in the silence, absorb the feeling, be thankful for already having it, not in your mind but feel it in your heart. Then watch for it to appear in your life as you know it is on its way with complete faith.

Silence enables discipline of thought and your thoughts change your lives. This is what is promised in the era of the new Renaissance as it was in many centuries gone by; your awareness of how you can create in your lives is to be found in the gift of silence.

How you can stop attracting the negative and instead have a fulfilled life of well-being and great purpose.

Silence is necessary to constantly connect to your soul centre and create from there. Any creation from soul cannot be anything other than acting out your mission, your purpose and learning you have come to do on earth, whether this may be to mother the next generation of caretakers of the earth. Whether it is to build the next homes for the homeless, whether it is to sing and generate loving emotions which connect people to their soul and in turn to their purpose. Whether it is to bake or create art, whether it is to expound the profound beauty of the earth.

Silence is great for silence sake, to rest, to relax, review and hold those you hold dear close in your hearts. Love your life, love and respect silence as much as you respect being busy, doing and acting.

Communication with self, to know who you are is essential, to this purpose and end, take time to find space and silence. With silence comes knowledge of self, peace and contentment and creation within your life. Listen... to the silence.

Meditation

Meditation is different to silence but the two are interconnected. Meditation could be considered as a certain practice done a certain way and has been practised this way in many religions for many centuries. It is a certain practice which sometimes puts people off starting and continuing to meditate. They concentrate on the practice; you should be sitting this way or that, breathing this way or that, breathing this way or that, but really meditating is a natural occurrence. When you learn anything you start perhaps by breaking down the steps in order to learn how to attain the goal. The act then becomes second nature. For instance, when you are learning to drive, your brain eventually takes over and you don't process all the parts of the act individually, and it becomes seamless.

Some people need these steps first in meditation but they are just steps. What has to be remembered is in fact meditation is a natural part of who we are. It is just allowing your mind to wander away from everyday tasks and set it free, to relax and connect to your soul and /or Source. It is a way to develop your reconnection to spirit. To remember the awareness you need to have of your spiritual side, your soul whilst living in your physical form.

Silence, space, time can be important factors for meditation, but truly it can also be two minutes quickly captured at a desk, a refreshing of spirit and of mind.

A reconnection with where your soul is at, an ongoing conversation with your soul which can be revisited whenever you so desire. It is simple, a beautiful refreshment. To really make a connection you need to practise. Repetition will improve speed, but do not overcomplicate or ritualise, keep the flow natural. Keep it personal, it is all about you and your reconnection to self, to your spiritual side, to Source, to your soul to help you, it is to encourage you to be disciplined in your thought processes which in turn create your life.

Just as we have spoken of positive thought patterns, we also have to learn to let go of our daily thought clutter. For a small part of the day reduce the information that is steaming through the mind. To learn to use the meditative state to raise your energy, your frequency and your consciousness, your connection to all and feed this revelation back into your conscious thought practice of your daily life, then add faith, conviction, to create a wonderful fulfilled life which offers you all your soul has designed for you and your physical lifetime right now.

Many of these practices are connected but they do not need long drawn out procedures and how to guides. It needs to be natural, individual, where you want to do it and when, part of your life for it is part of who you are, perhaps lighting a candle, sitting by the sea, watching a sunset. It is a connection through you to your higher self, to the earth, to humanity. Not a drawn out and long ritual but a natural part of who you are.

Love is a natural emotion. Meditation is a process of loving yourself to give yourself an escape from the hustle and bustle and really connect with your full self, why you are here and how you are going to choose to progress and move forward with your spiritual soul mission in your physical life now.

Meditation is not something to think only certain spiritual followers do; it is not to be thought as complicated. It is a dream state whilst you are awake, it is a relaxing of busy mind, and it is simple, natural method of being in touch with the real and whole you. You are always in the driving seat of your life. There is no wrong or right way to meditate, so this should not be a reason for you to feel you cannot begin.

Like many other learning tasks in life just begin, then improve, then learn, then think of it as second nature, for we are spirit first and body second though in this era of renaissance we are to become aware of how the two combine.

How the two together create the most wonderful forms for humanity and its growth.

You already work together, mind, body, spirit. The difference in the new renaissance will be that you aim and will be fully aware of how this works and so create in a more focussed and precise way.

Meditation can help your progress with this but do it in love, for yourself, ask for help, ask for guidance. Ask for that which you desire and have faith and allow receipt.

Meditation is a simple, natural way to find a re-connection with you but in a light-hearted and focussed way. Happy meditating! Enjoy connecting to who you truly are.

Welfare

Your welfare in life, what keeps you well, in order, how you run your everyday life is dependent upon your thoughts. Your awareness of your higher frequency, energy, consciousness is important for the realisation on a personal level that you are a spiritual being in a physical body.

The spiritual and physical are interconnected and so the welfare and well-being of your body in everyday life is dependent on the quality of the creations you make for yourself in your life and this is in turn dependent upon the thoughts you choose and the choices you make.

There are thousands of thoughts which pass through your brain every day, 50,000 or more. You choose which thoughts you think in passing, new thoughts about new experiences happening to us and around us. The thoughts can even slip into the mind seemingly without a glance but they are all choices and all your responsibility.

The thoughts which are important to our welfare are the ones that are turned over again and again, the ones repeated to ourselves in inner dialogue, the ones revisited and held in faith with conviction. It is this conviction and faith in our own thoughts about ourselves and others which is the link to our welfare in our daily lives. Simply we are giving energy to the thoughts we mull over and over and this sets the process of our subconscious working to bring those things we give energy to, into our lives, and so ultimately physically materialises them into our every day.

So we need awareness of our thoughts and the subconscious part of ourselves which gives suggestion to conscious mind and then add faith, energy and conviction to this and you have a formula for creation into your life. To achieve then a life that is full of well-being, health and abundance it begins with these intentions in mind and choosing these sorts of thoughts and adding energy and action to them with behaviour in line with those thoughts.

If you concentrate on the negative, worry, anxiety and give it energy, time, repetition and faith that you are right in it all being negative and convinced it will always be so. Then you are generating more of the same into your life through this subconscious pattern through to manifestation into your world, your reality, your everyday lives.

So, the task in this new era of awareness, of the Renaissance, is indeed to become aware of our thoughts and how we process them and more importantly how we can direct them to achieve the experience we want in life, the one your soul has come to earth to have.

Look at the negative, accept it, solve it or if it is out of your control then let it sit a while. Then allow any energy you have surrounding it to go, replace it with some positive thought that all will be well in the end and be at peace with it. Give no energy or repeated thought to it, just let go of the worry and anxiety around it, deal instead with it in a matter of fact attitude. It is here, I accept it, I can do this about it and do it, or leave it if it is out of your hands and surround the situation with positive energy.

Imagine a filing system, an inbox, an acceptance tray and a letting go tray. Non-attachment to the problem doesn't mean you bury your head in the sand and don't deal with it. It means by treating it in a different way you can stop giving increasing energy to the negative, and instead, concentrate on the positive, treat it with the positive. Enable the energy of your thoughts to be processed in a way that you are not adding fuel to the fire instead you are dampening the flames with positive choices. Many of human anxieties and problems are not so large when broken down in this way because the mind is not then running away with all the millions of possibilities that could happen. Instead you are controlling those thoughts, releasing anxiety and stress and encouraging your own well-being and welfare towards positive goals.

Therefore, the way our thoughts are processed and our awareness of their power means that we can be consciously aware and disciplined about the thoughts we hold in conviction and faith and the way we hold the well-being and welfare of our lives in our own hands.

It is an important aspect of the new era that we stop looking outside of ourselves for solutions to our problems. Instead we need to seek and find the tools we were given to enable us to create in a positive way in our lives for our own well-being and this in turn has an effect on the people immediately close to us and those further afield.

Our own welfare is not down to government or others around us instead solutions are to be found in self first, awareness first, developing our natural tools, power of thought. Creating new experiences in our lives from a position of being in our power, from choice that all humanity has available to them, this is the way forward. Blaming those outside of us defeats us because it means they have control over us and our thoughts.

We seem to desire freedom and choice, we attribute our losses in life to others, yet we do not see we already have choice and the freedom we demand of governments and those in power. We give away our power in a sense for in the pattern of blame we have made them responsible, and if they are responsible, it means they have made choices on our behalf and we have denied ourselves that duty of choice for fear of having the responsibility.

The choice and freedom which all humanity has is within, through own thought, choices made about self-for-self and so this is how we should begin to understand what tools we have. 50,000 thoughts a day needs discipline, it needs direction, faith and conviction. I am in perfect health. I will learn accounts. I will learn to swim. I can do... I will take the first step to... I will find out how to... Choice in your head first, positive choice, I will walk once a week and save my bus fare towards that course and get fitter by walking... I can volunteer my time in a charity shop and learn how to dress a window... I can... I will... I am able to... Always positive, even the slightest thought.

Choice has always been ours and always will be. Of course we can choose to stay the same, do the same and ultimately the results you get will be the same. If you challenge yourself, without excuses or blame on others, if you choose a better experience, do something more positively the world will work with you.

Choose to do something for your own welfare, do something differently and you will get a different result. It is universal law. The outcome is relative to what has been put into the system, an energy exchange. Negative thought, focussing on the problem, giving energy to it, will bring about negative experience. The soul which just lives for experience, responds to the energy and where it is directed and so chooses energetically more of that experience until you, the human aspect, the mind has a chat to the soul and says, "Stop we want a different experience now."

Instead replace the inner dialogue. "Let's have a more positive experience, let's have a problem-free day, and yes, let's do that for a change that is what I choose." Then get some really good energy behind that choice, believe it, have faith in it with great conviction. Feel how great that day is going to be and when that day is done and it was great, do it again and make bigger and better choices. Now this takes practise because your mind will be having lots of dialogue saying, "Oh but we always do this" and want to pull you back into old, comfortable easy choices, where you don't have to work thinking of new experiences but if you stand fast and keep trying even when you find it hard, it will work.

Your welfare is in your hands. Focus on the solution, a better experience, even better imagine the solution or better experience. Better still, imagine it with energy, faith and full conviction as if it is already there, feel it, allow your soul to know that it is your choice. Do not let your conscious mind get in the way with all the different outcomes. Do not consider what would happen if this went wrong or allow doubt in. This diffuses the energy. Instead have faith and conviction of your choice and have focus. Where there is doubt, there is no true conviction and faith.

Therefore, the power of thought alongside its true conviction and faith equals ability to bring new experience into daily life and enables true well-being and welfare well-managed by self-for-self.

One Thought

One thought concentrated on the negative can lead to a multitude of negatives in your lifetime, in your pattern of thinking and reality.

Imagine then that you train yourself to look out for just one positive thought. We have many thoughts in a day and if our pattern is to stay in the stream of negative inner dialogue then all sorts of troubles will be manifested into our life in accordance with the energy and focus and conviction we give to that one root thought.

So chase it back to the one root thought. Search for a new thought, a better thought and set a wider light on the thoughts you choose and discard ones that will not hold true with what you want to attract into your life.

Go far back. Is your thought about dignity and respect, or is it based in resentment? Is it based in not being worthy and not loved, or is it based in I can't, I don't know? Then maybe it is time to see that we have the solution in our hands. We have to open our eyes, ears and hearts and minds to see how our conscious mind and subconscious and our physical body, our mind, body, soul are really connected. Time to understand we create and have created the reality in our lives. It is all based on our thought patterns derived from our ingrained beliefs brought about by the acceptance of many influences throughout our lives.

It is a wonderful thing that humanity is so diverse. We have many difficulties in our lives sometimes because of this. We look always for solutions outside ourselves. We give reason why we do the things we do and why we cannot achieve our goals. We even on occasion find others to blame.

We are unlikely to search in the very place where the difficulties arise because we are unaware in terms of our consciousness exactly how this trouble, has appeared in our lives. We need to start looking inward. The idea is simple, not a complicated journey of many years finding yourself, but it is as challenging, if not more so. It is challenging because it asks you to open and pick at a belief system you were essentially born into.

This is not an opportunity to blame this condition; it was an aspect of your own choice which was chosen before you came to this earth. It was chosen for a purpose only your soul knows and is guiding you to achieve. The experience it wants your human physical aspect to have.

Your feelings and your navigation system can offer you contact with this purpose. *What feels right is right.* What does not is not. This changes over time and so you are guided. What was right at one time may be different in the now. The obstacles in your way however lie in your own belief system.

It is therefore important to bring into your own awareness how one thought, one deep rooted, simple yet powerful thought, the one you always come back to through all difficult situations, the one repeated over and over building up its power making the obstacle, the wall to climb, thicker, deeper, higher, the one thought which is so rooted that it colours all other beliefs and opportunities is the thought you have chosen for yourself.

The process of choosing may be due to outside influences of upbringing, schooling, religious doctrine, all sorts of environmental possibilities. These influences have not been the party to blame for there is no blame to be had. It is just a simple non-awareness of how powerful your thoughts are and how they are a tool for you to use and create with. Your soul may have chosen a certain life experience to have and the environment in which that happens but you always have the power of choice to change those circumstances. It is a gift, a wonderful gift from your God (or science or whatever, or whoever you choose to believe in or not) a gift nonetheless.

Now the thought has built in power over time. You may have been told you were trouble, or not academic, or fat or thin or not worthy or selfish or not lovable… the words, thoughts and beliefs are limitless, there is power in them in that they are limiting, *particularly if they are negative and you have chosen to accept them as true*. If you then go on to nurture them, cosset them as yours, and you choose to hold onto them they become who you think you are, they become your story. You may bury them away in your subconscious mind or leave them openly in your conscious mind.

Then your conscious mind is attracted to the same energy of these thoughts and seeks to find further evidence, perhaps a more recent situation that supports these negative thoughts. Your behaviour then goes back to I can't do that because of what went before or what and who you are defined by from the earlier thoughts. Never realising the limiting thoughts you have buried and embedded are your only true obstacle. You may have added other thoughts now which add further to this limiting belief about yourself and so a negative pattern builds.

So the conscious mind feeds the subconscious with more facts and experiences from the senses, experienced through this limited belief pattern. Your subconscious works on suggestions made to it and so then its job is to take a simple suggestion and listen to those offered with faith and conviction whether it is negative or not—it doesn't stipulate. Subconscious takes suggestion, faith and conviction a feeling energy if you will and then delivers that right to your front door, into your life into your physical reality.

In other words, thought, even one thought, offered with faith and conviction has power. There are universal laws governing with intention and protecting you from directly harming others. You cannot harm another without first harming yourself. However, we are looking at how your choosing patterns are established. So go back, look back to the deep rooted thoughts that set these patterns in motion and that you use to justify the reality of your life.

Look at your inner dialogue, look inward at what you are blaming, what you accepted that was suggested to you, whose judgement of who you are you chose to live up to. Look at what you want from life and accept responsibility for your thoughts from now on. If a deep rooted thought appears to be an obstacle in what you want to experience, then simply change the thought, find

75

a new positive appropriate thought, add faith and conviction to it and build a new experience.

You have the ability to change your thoughts. Say goodbye to the old ones not working for you. Replace them, redecorate your inner dialogue and renew yourself with faith and conviction these are essential, for it is the energy of faith and conviction in the new thought which will change your circumstances. In this way change of your outer world comes from within. Change has to come from the thoughts you choose and accept. This new beginning can start with one thought.

Revenge/War

We must look at this subject, but we may think well that is a very negative title. What is going to be said about war and hate and revenge? After all, there is surely nothing positive which can come out of that. Well, my friends it is part of the challenge of humanity not to pre-judge. War has existed on the earth for centuries. It has been seen as a solution to many disputes of power, control and part of the human way. It has been derived from fear, fear of loss, of possessions, homes, fear of others hurting those we hold dear, fear of losing our values and who we deem ourselves to be. It is a decree of absolution, that we are protecting the lands our forefathers fought for. It is a power battle with our past and with what we deem to be right. To uphold the respect of our ancestors who have gone before and even in the name of the future we plan for our families. There are many reasons for war.

Yet war can bring no real solutions to fear of loss. For the reality of it is that we cannot achieve lasting results from hurting our enemies with that which they have done to us. Even when it is a show of power it is a show of fear at the core of it. We cannot cure fear by killing. All that fear continues long after the killing is done unless it is addressed at its root source.

There is a point where our energies will be hurt by the negativity we wish or act upon each other. Let us find an alternative way. It is important to see a higher energy, a higher consciousness in these matters. For this reality is true, the earth is borrowed by us and lent to us. We are able to create what we need when we desire it and so nothing is permanent for we are here to learn our lessons and have our chosen soul experiences, and in these overcome our challenges to learn from relationships with those we share the earth with. War and revenge makes us stay in a moment where we are hard done by. It makes us stuck in battles often perpetuated from long ago; stuck in feelings passed down from one generation to another. Desire for power and control in essence come from fear of loss.

War is sought in justification of one power being higher than another, of one people being better than another and in one belief system being better than another.

Yet we should be seeking to see the similarities which may be the love of our children and families. We all have that in us and embracing diversity, to play to people's strengths and allow learning from this. We all laugh, we all cry, we all die in this world, now we should experience life together in peace. Embrace the meeting point that is the same. We are all human and all hurt, all love. It is in this time of 100 years since the First World War that we remember that even in the deep midst of war men stopped to acknowledge each other.

Where does this fit in with this era of more conscious awareness. The human part of the spirit enables us to see, this, the great resilience, the great empathy and compassion of seeing our enemy in the same position as ourselves with the same possibility of loss of family, values and what we hold dear. We have in a sense in the moment connected with the essential spirit of our enemy and recognised the meeting point of that which is the same as us.

We are all connected in spirit and so when we hurt someone else we cannot avoid hurting ourselves. It is inevitable. The way we think of others on a day to day basis perhaps not with revenge but with resentment or wanting to hurt back, to make them pay in some way will only change our own energy.

Our energy of higher consciousness is connected with love and love of our families who have been hurt makes us quick to anger and want to hurt back. This however lowers our own frequency, our energy and so then can only attract to us by universal law that which is present on this lower energy level. So it is a downward spiral as more negativity attracts to us and we concentrate more and more of the negative feelings towards our enemies.

A letting go of the feeling which is connected to the situation, when you let go and release it to a higher consciousness, offers a possibility of seeing it in a different perspective, and this will allow a rebalancing of your energy to heal and move forward not forgetting but living in a level of energy which will allow you to rise to the learning. Learning need not be repeated over and over again and certainly not with the consequences of war.

There are no winners in war of course. The war that wages within afterwards kills the spirit, and it reduces energy and takes the individual away from soul purpose. There is no judgement in this. Only energy generated and attracted and repeated.

Old energy needs to be released and in the new era of renaissance we should be free to choose a different way, a pathway of peace and care and contentment and of course love. This is what humanity craves. If fear is the root cause of many disputes, war and revenge then the answer is simply love, for love conquers fear always.

So maybe the need for war is explained by the need for its opposite, the desire for the solution and without it we cannot find the solution we seek, the ultimate love which is valued after the devastation war leaves behind. So can we find the solution, the way forward to love our fellow humans without the harsh lesson of war to bring us to that point?

Those that have died in war and passed back to their spirit home are offered the opportunity to form an army in a different way, a light army working for humanity towards peace which they value greatly, a way without loss.

History has shown us war devastates; therefore, our intellect needs to take charge with our soul's humanity and learn the evolved position without the physical lesson. It needs no repetition. *Be at peace with yourselves first and the rest of the world next.*

Awareness

What is the purpose of this era of new consciousness, the new Renaissance? It is to bring about change of belief, change of awareness, a higher consciousness, and a realisation of what mankind is, to lift humanity, for it is greatly loved. It is a wonderful place, earth and its people, a wonderful creation. The development and evolution of humanity never stops. Life always keeps going despite the challenges and the earth keeps spinning. Beliefs are constantly updating, in technology new information comes along and perspective through the senses shifts. It shifts at a fantastic rate and of course it gets faster as technology changes. Beliefs, thoughts, and energy exchanges can be shifted in seconds and a new belief stirred and created.

Awareness understands your spiritual side; it is about understanding who you are within the context of your physical life. It is about combining the two, the spiritual and the physical, so that the choices of thought, the words spoken and therefore the creations in your life come from a place of awareness, knowing who you are. That it comes from your soul, the place within, which gets so overlooked when we are absorbed living our lives.

Awareness is not about climbing some spiritual or even religious ladder though some structured paths may help some as a stepping stone. There are various ways to awareness. It is instead a way of being, a decision, and a conscious decision to pay heed to that which really drives you and who is really in the driving seat, to pay heed to your soul. It is for you to decide that there is more to you than the challenges of everyday life. To be aware that there is a chance for you to create wonderful experiences in your life by learning and acknowledging just how you really work.

Humanity goes through life searching for so much outside of itself and forgets to search inside instead.

We ignore what is before us and this is where we need to make a change. This is where humanity can be reborn and evolve its thinking, speaking and creating. Life on earth can be full of joy, love and contentment. It can be driven forward on these feelings of love and cooperation rather than driven from fear. Many push through fear and face challenges, but many are overwhelmed by fear consciously. Some use this fear to control others, as they see the power of it and use manipulation. The inner self of choice and free will is weakened. Some drive forward their plans in life not even knowing that subconsciously it is fear driving the decisions. Then they wonder why the outcome is an uneven road when fear is the master.

If one thought is changed, the root thought and if you focus on the solution rather than the problem, if you become aware that the way you think is the key to your life reality then it can be seen that it is the change in awareness which holds the real power for humanity and its future.

Awareness of self, awareness of soul, awareness of spirit above and in physical life below, awareness of how it is all connected, awareness of the joining of the two worlds, acknowledging that you are a living breathing spirit as well as a living body, all of this is being truly aware of yourself. Living with awareness of your soul's perspective as well as the physical body's perspective, AS WELL AS, and so bringing about a fulfilling and meaningful life for yourself and your families and for humanity as a whole.

Awareness starts with the individual, it starts from inside out. It starts with a search that knows no other way than to come from the soul. It is the soul, life, connection. We need to connect to our souls, our passions, our gifts. We need to look face on and with soul for the true purpose for existing in the physical realms. Our soul knows. Each individual soul knows the reason. If we do not connect to this inner being we will be forever searching, often in the wrong place.

Within our interactions we need to learn to come from the heart, from a base of love, the soul of us, to think the best of ourselves as individuals and connected humanity. We need to do this without arrogance, without fear, without undervaluing.

We have to enjoy our own self-worth and learn self-love; we need to take to others our best from a point of self-assurance we find in this new awareness. Not to compete with it, but to share and be with it and in this way, we offer a healing to others.

It is a healing of the spirit by simply enabling them to find this power in themselves. It is a passing on from one soul to another, enabling, empowering, and a powerful chain of awareness.

Awareness that a change in your thinking, awareness in the power of your soul, your passions, your gifts all of this is the way you can move forward.

The physical life is a challenge to help your soul learn. It is in this way a privilege, and it is always an opportunity for your soul's gifts to take place in physical reality. It is an opportunity to develop these talents and enable and empower and connect others too to the love they hold in their soul and create with it into their physical 'being'. This awareness begins with us. It begins with the individual, no one else is responsible but you, you are always in charge of who you are and you are responsible for that too.

It begins by taking a negative thought you are thinking, perhaps recognising at first that it is negative, about a situation, someone else or yourself following it back to where it started.

Then taking this thought, changing it, letting go of the negative feeling, creating a new more positive thought about it. Not just putting a sticking plaster on it but instead thinking and feeling with conviction a more positive outcome.

It has already been solved. It has created a new trail of energy, this new thought. The how is not important— that is not your focus. Your focus is to recognise the power of your thoughts, create new ways of being which serve you and your soul purpose in this world. Your soul purpose is always connected to other people on the earth as we are all connected so to be your true self is about feeling self-love, self-worth and then spreading that in your own unique way for the benefit of the whole. You cannot achieve it alone, yet you must start from within.

So after you have reached the new thought, imagine the positive outcome and have faith and conviction it will be, is already here. For time is relative. It is done. This is the power of positive thought. This is the gift of humanity. All we are missing is the awareness of why we can do this, the realisation that we have a part of God; Source within us, our God self, the awareness that we create our reality from our souls connected to Source from a point of love. Without this awareness of our true inner being, our soul and connecting to it every day we are missing out on an essential part of us. We must begin to be consciously aware of who we really are.

Health

Health is not just your body's wellness, though importance of good food, good sleep, and good exercise is paramount. True health is all about balance between your emotional body, your mind and your physical body too. It is about making sure this connection between all of these is in balance. You are more than your physical body. It is important you care for this vessel as it then enables you to keep the energy of your spirit in balance and at a higher frequency and greater awareness. With greater frequency comes higher energy for your body too. It is a balance. The human spirit is a great part of you and capable of wondrous acts as long as it comes from a point of well-being and great balance and with this balance strength of being.

Health starts in the mind. Your thoughts and focus and positive thoughts can aid any malady. Doctors should be consulted, of course, as positive thought is not used instead of medicine, but it aids recovery because it enables the restoring of balance of energy within the body. Positive thinking enables a higher frequency which in turn allows the medicine to work at a higher rate and for balance between energetic bodies and the physical body to be restored.

If you focus on thoughts of what is wrong with you rather than the goal of good health and healing, then you will get a slower journey back to health. If you choose the path of positive thought, it enables you to heal quicker, feel uplifted.

The spirit can be uplifted by the beauty of the arts, music, art, relaxation or beautiful landscapes. Life is full of beauty, joy and positivity and it will bring these forth in your healing dependent upon what you concentrate on. If you use the power of thought and you make the choice of health in your thoughts, you will feel better about yourself and so decide to eat well, exercise enough, look after yourself and make better choices because you value yourself. You feel worthy of good health and your own care and so you will attract care on the same level from others.

What you give out you receive back in abundance. Health then starts in your thoughts but is maintained in physical reality. It is your responsibility to take care of your thoughts and your spirit and your body. If you worry too much, if you resent, regret or are stressed and anxious these negative thoughts which accumulate in your emotional body then can influence what happens in your physical body. They are all connected and we must start to become aware of this connection and balance our food, exercise, relaxation but also the way we think about ourselves, about our bodies.

Health is a connection; it is a way of mind and a following up with physical action. It is individual too. It is our responsibility to go to doctors when we need to, look after all of our individual needs.

Health care is a prominent issue within society on earth and where the future lies is the ability to take responsibility for our own health first and this is about right thought and right action.

We must see food as medicine, the nutrients within, it is not good letting others determine whether we are the right size, the right shape or the right look. We have to start from within, the beauty within, the diamond that is the soul, revealing the true beauty of you and then keeping true to yourself in the way you express yourself and look after your body.

Your food contains nutrients which are needed to keep the body and function of the mind well and healthy. Some food is enjoyed as a treat and that is a part of the joy of life, a little wine, a little treat, a little music, enjoy the wonders of the earth but in all things a little balance.

Be kind to your body generally and it will be kind to you. Health and well-being is not about excesses and deprivation instead it is about care, compassion and love for yourself in the way YOU care for your emotions, your body and your mind.

When all of these are in balance, health and life is simple but it is about being consciously aware of what you put in your body and what that is doing for it. It is important to eat these nutrients every day and keep your eyes well and your heart fit.

A little fish, a little bread, a little oil, a little wine, fresh fruits and vegetables and sunshine nutrition to be at your best; it is very important. The spirit should be uplifted by walking and contemplating beautiful countryside or scenery that you love. Music and art is very therapeutic, looking at it, experiencing it and making it. To support and feel supported are all factors in good health, enjoying company of good friends and laughing with them. Food, joy, relaxation, love, music and meditation, laughter are all the medicine of humanity. The simplicity of health starts before troubles come along, maintaining positive mental attitude creates positive energy in healing.

Medical experts are needed as well, no-one here is professing you do without them, quite the opposite. A broken limb still needs looking after but what we as humans can do is love the sore limb. Have positive thoughts that it is healing quickly and is a strong repair.

To allow healing not rushing it but loving yourself as a whole not just a body thus creates an atmosphere of love of self, of self-compassion of care and positivity for self that will create a higher frequency for the healing to take place.

Health then is in our hands and our minds; it is our responsibility. It is about honouring the medical professions but adding to it a holistic view of mind and spirit as well as the body. We can take control of the way we look at our health, perhaps *prevention in this way IS better than cure* and our society on earth will have the resources for those needing more help, more compassion, more love and care.

Health is a gift, a gift we must cherish and maintain and it is a precious gift we must take responsibility for.

Creation

It is a wonderful thing creation, not just creation of the earth, the beauty of the world, humanity itself by the creation of individual souls and in turn the creation each individual soul creates for themselves in their lives.

Of course sometimes this goes astray. The mechanism which individual souls create is not always fully understood and so they find themselves in a reality which is not what they would want to create for themselves but indirectly have through their own thoughts. It is sometimes hard to receive that information that we can create for ourselves even the challenges, obstacles and difficulties in our reality. We certainly do and we can create such a cycle of events that it becomes difficult to get ourselves free of it. Everything may feel as if it is weighing us down, that nothing is going our way and then we feel stuck. How do we get ourselves out of this "stuckness"? Who do we turn to, to help us?

Where is the solution? The answer eludes us many times because we misunderstood our own tools, our gifts, and our power as a human being.

Creation of individual souls, unique beings making up a whole we as humanity are an expression of God, Source, Creator... It is a part of God which exists within us and this divine self, the God self, a spark within us all is connected to our physical self just as much as our arms and legs are attached to our bodies. We are more than our physical bodies. We have said this before and it is a reality.

The creation upon the earth has been an evolution, a development to enable souls to experience, experience through the ages, new experiences based on what has gone before but stretching out to what is new. There have been bottles of power, of religion, politics, of learning, developments of language, thoughts, art, music, communications, technology and human rights.

Just look back for a moment over the history and the development of man. What was developed, changed, studied, in just the last 100 years? In the last 500 years? In the last 1000 years? Humanity is always evolving, it is inevitable and with it values of society also change. The time is changing now, there is a new evolution. A new beginning, as I call it from my time on the earth, with such beauty yet alongside such conflict in order for change. Today, like then, this time, this era is a time of a new renaissance, a rebirth with humanity's creation. An evolution where all that has been learned emotionally, music, art, sculpture, poetry, writing, creativity to touch the spirit and move the emotions of humanity forward, to light up feelings of love, warmth, compassion, empathy, and to stir the emotions. This evolution compounds all that has been learned intellectually to help us again to move forward but in a different way.

In the 1400-1500s many scholars had words written in the Greek and Latin languages at their fingertips but ordinary man could not understand the written word. Today we click a button. Many languages have developed and are available to us. Technology has moved forward and medicine, science, and everyday tasks are carried out by machines. The learning is enormous. We take it as everyday developments but humanity has moved forward in enormous leaps.

Spiritually humanity is a little behind in its development. When life was simpler and in some senses more physically demanding then spiritually people were perhaps more aware of something outside of themselves. In this era the fear factor was great. They believed that God, Gods, had all the power and so how they behaved meant a journey to heaven or hell. They had a connection between their spiritual beliefs and their daily lives.

Sadly, men of power and politics used this to their own ends in certain times and so fear became part of spiritual beliefs and religious doctrine. Whether this was correct thinking or not, it was how it worked in the context of those times.

So throughout the ages humanity has had various learnings by individual souls, as a society and as humanity as a whole.

Exploration of the world in all realms, the physical, the emotional, the spiritual, this new era is about understanding this evolution of creation and connecting all three together, bringing who we are, our divine self, present in our soul, together with our reality of life and our connection to Creator, Source, God.

In turn bringing about a new respect of self, a respect of who we are and how we operate in the world. This renaissance, this evolution, this creation will be magnificent as long as humanity understands that it all begins with self. So back to the question of whom shall we go to help us when we are in "stuckness"? Who will solve our problems? What is the solution and where will I find it? The answer is SELF, the self who has understood creation, its purpose, the self who no longer denies the God-self within. However, you are not alone in this—you are never alone.

Let me explain a little more. We all have the ability to create what is in our world. So let us look at individual creation. Everything that is created in matter, physical substance started at first as a thought. A thought somebody has chosen, it may be connected to a feeling, or it could be a design, a question in science. It may simply be how to approach the day. The power of thought is unlimited. The choice of thought is only limited by your own belief system.

Your environment may have created obstacles in early life, however, you have the choice how you let them influence you. You can choose to make them a positive experience, a learning of resilience, of a knowing of what you don't want in your life, a learning how to create something different. You can choose to keep them as your limiting beliefs and you can decide that you can't do this because of that or you can be brave, courageous and be truly creative. You can leave behind the negative and start a new small renaissance for you. A rebirth of attitude, but that is not to say you just walk away and drop everything. It is more to do with your thoughts, a rebirth of your approach, of your thoughts and what you create for yourself—a new beginning. It starts and finishes with you. Your divine self, your physical, spiritual and emotional self can choose a new beginning by choosing at that beginning simply a new thought.

Each thought brings a new creation, a creation which will spark another. Change many negative thoughts by repeating positive ones around the subject and watch what unfolds and is created in your physical reality. Of course there is more to it than that. We are changing your belief patterns which have been creating your stumbling blocks in life. Instead think positive, choose positive, believe and have FAITH in the positive without question, yes without question, feel it with all your being, know it, love it, be that positive thing, give positive energy to it, feel and bathe in the positive energy of it. It is this which will create the positive in physical world and into physical matter, in substance, in relationships, in opportunities of your desires appearing in your life.

POSITIVE THOUGHT WITH FULL FAITH AND CONVICTION EQUALS CREATION.

The conviction is in the energy you give it and that can be a physical action towards it as well.

We are souls able to create individually and also because we then make positive change in our own little world it extends outwards and makes positive change in the world.

Evolution stretches outwards and humanity's values change positively. It begins and ends with each individual becoming aware of God's creation, us, being able to create in his world, in his service for the purpose of soul and humanity evolution. You are not alone in this creation.

Whichever God you connect with or if you connect with none, there is an individual evolution in this creation, to connect with God, to create peace, contentment, compassion and love in your own lives and so in the lives of those dear to you and to the family of humanity itself.

In this way creation is a reflection of your own soul and the expression of the connection you have to each other, the family that is humanity. Creation is a gift of God. Creation is within your experience. We have to learn to use it to better the world experience. We have to use the gifts we have, we have to realise our connection to God and bring about the next evolution of humanity, one where spirit, body and mind work together in creative harmony.

Body

You are living your reality in your physical vessel, your body. This is not all you are. You are not just a physical body; you have an emotional body, an ethereal body and much more. Here we are concentrating on the physical body. Your soul chooses this body you are using, it chooses what it needs for its journey and experience on this earth and it chooses what it needs for its purpose of service and learning this time.

This said we often feel that our bodies are letting us down in some way. They have ailments, little things which mean they don't perform as we would wish. However, we are often letting our bodies down, not the other way around.

To keep healthy, strong and able to do our work, our learning, our developing our purpose in life we must first feed our bodies with the nutrients which it deserves. The nutrients it needs to perform and function in the physical world. Too many times the "desired" look is determined by society and this may lead to all aspects of misunderstanding the physical body and its optimum health.

Firstly we are all unique and this includes in stature and metabolism. We have to understand how our body can achieve its best health. Some may need more protein; some do very well on vegetables alone. It is not the case of one method of nutrition fits all. It is about the nutrients that will be best for that particular body. There are basic nutrients we all need. It is about eating for health and for the good of your body. It is about being able to love yourself as you are and give your body the best it can have.

Too much is eaten that has no value to the body; too much is wasted that has value. It is also about enjoyment, joy, flavour and treating food as medicine and fuel for the body.

Many ancient healing methods simply use natural herbs and nutrients from foods. Ill health is sometimes caused by a deficiency or absence of these minor nutrients. If you eat well, you heal well. A healthy body does not find ill health, instead it resonates on an energy level of being healthy. It knows it is well and attracts more energy frequency of being well.

As we have spoken before, it is also a matter of balance between the body and the mind. Thinking wellness gives you a high energy for your body and so it will not attract lower energies of viruses. However, when your body has a serious condition, medical help is required but your part is to keep thinking positive and working in harmony with the medical treatment by telling your body too that you are getting well, becoming well, and being well and that the treatment is the best it can be in balance with your body at that time.

So there is a connection between the body and the mind and also the soul for the soul chooses the purpose and all that it needs to do the job of learning and evolving here on the earth in a physical body.

Some bodies it seems have many difficulties and classed as disabled but of course it is a hard thing to accept that the soul within may have chosen this position in this physical life.

Let us briefly look at this, my friends, for it has to be dealt with great compassion and love. The souls within who have chosen this are some of the most courageous souls within existence for they know they have much to face and still they do it. They have much prejudice to battle against and much difficulty to overcome yet they come to teach. To teach us compassion, to teach us not to presume or assume, to teach us to value all souls, to teach us the beauty within regardless of the outward appearance, to teach us that we are all connected, all valuable and that all have beautiful gifts to offer to the world.

Viewing a body as incapable limits not only the person with the, shall we say, difference but also limits those with the beliefs that view them with a prejudiced eye. We are learning in this era. We have seen the capabilities of those injured in wars and this has been seen with great feats to the poles of the world against the natural challenges of weather. This shows great resilience, heart and fortitude but it also shows that no man can be judged by their appearances alone. We have seen the wonderful achievements of the para-Olympians. We are moving forward slowly we understand more; we are more loving and accepting more but there is still much to do.

Bodies are a vessel for the soul to experience life on earth and to express that soul, it is a wonderful gift. We therefore have to look after our body to enable it to hold the soul at an energy level it deserves.

It is part of our responsibility of humanity for an individual to look after its body and take care that the soul is encapsulated in a body, loved, a body fit for its purpose. It is part of you but only a part not the whole. It is about connection of mind, body and soul and so body is part of this, an important part and we have to love it, care for it and empower others to do the same. Our bodies are a wonderful part of our experience. We need to look as individuals how to best serve our bodies in order to work together as a connected whole. To recognise the important role a healthy body plays in the experience of being human. We are soul first but the body is our beloved temporary home.

Choice

The choice, my friends, is always with you, just as God is always with you whether you know, feel or connect with him or not. Choice of thoughts, choice of action, and choice of purpose are always down to the individual soul. Your obstacles have been self-made and you have the choice to remake them. It is hard to accept sometimes we know but the choice of thoughts which will make a difference to your present reality can be made in seconds, and if it is a more positive choice of thought and is held in faith and conviction, then things WILL change in a positive way.

Physical reality seems so immovable; the obstacles feel so firm and real that it seems incomprehensible that a move of thought, a choice of a new thought can move the obstacle. We have made our world from thought; it is the divine part of ourselves which we can use to provide for ourselves what God would wish for us.

This is always the best: all that we desire, all that we need and all for service. God has given us this gift yet we have become unaware of the power we have used against ourselves with the power of our own thought. We are caught up in the physical limitations and concentrate on the limitations and put energy to them, and then we manifest more of the limitation.

Instead choose to put your energy in the solution and not enter into the problem. Put faith into the positive solution as much as you would have into thinking of the problem over and over again.

Then allow it to be, accepting it will be without resistance, allow the solution to come into your life and let it happen. Have faith, release drama. Then let it all be, the how it will happen is not your part of the plan. Your part is to consciously look at the choices you are making, the choices of your thoughts, your actions and consequently your creations in your life.

The choice is always with you, always, it cannot be otherwise because you are a child of God and divine presence is a part of you and in so you create your own world from the point of that which you believe about yourself and others. If you change those beliefs and the choices you make, the outcomes will change with them. So be conscientious at looking at the way you think and what you choose. Look at the way and what you create and the way you look at yourself within your physical reality. Look at how you interact with others and what you think about them. Now, being consciously aware of your thoughts, your creations, does not mean that you have to monitor every thought and fear what will happen if you think one way or another. We are not in the business of generating fear here. No, we are in the business of making you very aware of your divine self and your ability to create the world God would want for you. There are really no limits only those you give yourself. We are also not in the business of misuse of this power. It has been done by so many generations, in ancient times and after.

Power, greed and position has in the past been the priority, this is concentrating on what is outside of self and ignoring peace, cooperation and compassion. There is a way to have enough, plenty and live in joy of giving in order to help others find this place of enough, plenty, joy, peace, security within self. All the things humanity desires and of course loves.

The drama of busy life in this world is created over and over in cycles from a place of fear of loss; a fear of not enough, this can then reveal itself in the form of greed and competition.

We are all unique and have unique gifts and purpose. No two people on this earth can fulfil their purpose in the same way because we are all a unique expression of God presence and creation in human form. We go through our lives, we choose to chastise or avoid instead of create a more positive alternative.

Set a positive thought in motion about how companies operate and so see them having more moral value for their employees. Change comes from within. We always have a choice. Everyone on the earth exercises their choice of thoughts, at least 50,000 thoughts a day per person. Imagine the power if 50% of those were positive about yourself, about the world and create an upward spiral instead of a downward pit.

The beginning is always with you, the individual, always, your choice of thoughts enable you to create in the world. Your responsibility is to check your thoughts, adjust them, create a new belief if necessary, and change your world by the choices you make. Your choices you make are important.

The life you create is important dependent upon the choices you choose and the thoughts you choose.

Choice is yours, and it is a gift from God.

You are not limited. You are an expression of divine presence of God in a human vessel with the God given gift of choice and also free will but with these come responsibility. It offers you unlimited potential, some already know this and have used it and so seemingly had an easy, fulfilled and opulent life.

You could do so too for we do all deserve. Are you choosing a different way? Inspect your inner dialogue. What thoughts are you choosing?

What are you saying to yourself? What are you saying to others about who you are? And what you can do? You have a choice, so choose a different dialogue and have faith in it. You know how to have faith and energy in something for you often put all your energy into worry and the things that are not right about your life and blaming others for these challenges and mishaps.

The responsibility is yours, the choice is yours, always, so choose wisely and choose what you really deserve in your life. Take out the drama, the worry, focus upon the positive change, the thought pattern and remember always that you have the gift of choice.

Connection

We are all connected in consciousness to each other. Our souls all come to the earth with a choice to fulfil a purpose for the evolution of the individual but also because we are all connected in this cycle of life and rebirth, the evolution of humanity, for many individuals make the whole.

We are all an expression of God and his desire to seek out experience in physical domain.

We learn, we experience, we raise consciousness, and we evolve the soul and so move humanity forward. We need to look at the connection also within our daily lives. To be connected to our inner soul and work through our physical lives is important, to stay connected to our true selves and live in awareness that we are spirit as well as physical body.

Our body will one day wear out but we are living spirit today within that body yet our soul remains immortal and so can take all the learning it has achieved in physical life back to the spiritual home, once its physical life on earth no longer exists. So being connected consciously to the purpose of your soul and how it has chosen the life you live now can be seen with a new perspective upon it. It brings questions how shall we live in this way, in this era with purpose and with connection to our souls and therefore our divine self, enabling our service with God in the evolution of man. It seems unlikely that we can do this in our everyday lives, live this tall order, but we can, and it is only a shift in consciousness required. A shift in how we approach the world. There are many people who accomplished wonderful and elaborate things in life and some who achieve what appears simple, but all is valuable, it is about perspective. To achieve the goals, you have set out to do there must be connection to the part of you that chose those goals and a connection to the reason for those choices.

There is a shift from the physical focus to the spiritual focus, bringing you back in the physical realm and focus in everyday life, but with a new reason, a new perspective, or rather an old ancient connection that has always been but a new realisation of it, a new era of realisation that we are connected to God and our souls and each other and that with this connection we are in the driving seat of our lives. We are people with unlimited potential who can move forward to achieve goals we never thought we could achieve.

As we then become aware of this connection, and can overcome our own personal limitations, we then rise up to become our best selves. This has a reflection on others we interact with and then a ripple effect.

A change in one person can make a huge difference as long as it is passed on in good faith and good intention and the connection with all souls in mind, treating all with compassion and with guidance to a greater awareness.

Connection on an individual basis with God is important whichever religion you follow or if you don't follow any a connection to the source which feeds the spirit within. Religious doctrine is a pathway to the connection, the wire; you provide the plug and are responsible for plugging into God in faith. So the divine spark, God-self, or the divine presence in yourself allows you to steer through your challenges with new thought and faith in your divine self. Then your connection to God makes your life better and achieves your goals and your soul's mission.

There are two ways to exist in the world: connected and not. Yet we are all really connected to God, and it is inevitable as each soul is imparted from and with part of the divine presence. What differs is the level of recognition of this by each individual. Having no recognition of this divine connection does not make that individual separate from that divine presence, instead it just means they are just not so aware of it that is all. The task then is to become aware.

Each individual soul has work to do. Each individual alive has a soul and therefore we cannot escape from being connected to God. In this era, this new renaissance, we are endeavouring to help humanity to become mindful of its own lack of awareness of the connection to God. This era is about finding a way for each individual soul to realise who you are and how you have a wonderful relationship with God within yourself, by being you. This connection is ultimately your faith, faith in yourself and the divine presence that is within you, just in being you. One religion is not better than another in this. They are merely different paths for different individual souls to tread to make this connection back to God where the soul originated. The doctrine of religions is sometimes misunderstood or has had a misalignment with this truth. The doctrines were pathways set down earlier in a soul's evolution to enable humanity to explore a spiritual path, to understand there was more to them than the physical and to remind them of a connection to the divine presence in and around them in the beauty of creation itself. Doctrine in its own context of when each was first written or preached was often in troubled times when discipline was needed; an order was to be put in place to guide souls to something outside of themselves. Over the eras that have passed teachers, there were many, in many religions in many eras, who came to earth to guide in this, have been held up and revered and this is right to do so for they were wonderful souls offering the world great teachings, love, compassion and wisdom.

However, man has often taken the words, prayers, doctrines, lessons in a direction to have power over others. This has happened in all religions in many generations. This era of new renaissance tries to reveal that the teachings within all religions bring you back to your individual connection to God and you must be responsible for bringing about God's wishes for mankind to experience peace, joy, abundance, compassion and love for all people, in his own soul. To do this through your strong connection, your faith, spark of divine presence that God gave you with the gifts of choice and free will to choose a pathway in your physical and spiritual development to love, peace and renewal of spirit on this earth. Connection to your true self, connection to your soul, connection to God and ultimately, connection to each other — WILL achieve peace everlasting.

Courage

Courage to live is more important than the courage to die. We live in order to experience but it takes courage to live from who we truly are, from the soul. Many who are tackling terminal illness know this battle and the courage it takes to live each day. The perspective of what is truly important in life, what you love and live for crystallises when time is limited. The depth of living becomes entwined, cocooned within simplicity; the simple pleasures in life, for often the more complicated pleasures cannot be achieved. The will decides that the importance is to live from the soul from who you truly are to experience the moment in its fullness. The courage to do so is great. To be that courageous, to really live in the face of death enables us to see how to live when death is not lurking at the door.

So we should strive to live from this example without the need for the challenge to bring us to this learning. We should live in the now, in fullness, for no-one knows when it will be our time to return home. The limit on our life is unknown; however the quality of life and the courage to fully live it is unlimited.

We have full potential to use our courage at all times to live our lives to the full now, before the moment our challenges become extreme, and courage to live our lives, steering from the soul, accomplishing that which we are able to do and that which we have come to do.

Love is our most important treasure and it is courage to find it, seek it, share it, give it and receive it which makes life worthwhile.

How courageous it is to love when faced with adversity, when faced with animosity and when we think we cannot forgive. Courage sees you through, without courage we find our challenges unsurmountable but to take a deep breath and find heart and love when the "chips are down" reveals true courage.

How to have courage when all one feels is desolation and despair is a leap of faith. To close ones eyes and move forward, to smile, to feel faith and gain strength is the way to find courage to see you through. Many find it hard to feel this courage and many do not know the courage they store deeply inside. Humanity IS courageous beyond belief when real courage is required, you can see this in everyday situations. The courage of a child with cancer raising money for other children, the Mother who cares for their dying child, a parent who looks after their disabled child day in and day out. Caring, sharing, and loving in the face of ultimate challenge. Life is in need of courage, it also needs love. It also needs acknowledgement of what is important, the experience of now, living for the moment with joy in your heart, no worry for next year or moment beyond. Full experience of the now, that takes courage. Courage to live your goals and courage to empower those you hold dear to follow their passions, to sort out a path for themselves that leads to happiness in the moment of now.

Courage of fathers to show their feelings to their sons so they learn emotion is not a weakness, courage to stand up for your true beliefs without hurting your fellow man. Loving and learning with cooperation. Creating community with courage and daring to follow your heart even if it means facing admonishment. Have courage to face your fears and work through them and to stand in your power. Have courage to care about your world and your fellow man. Courage above all else to be yourself and live before you die (physical death). Be courageous and live life to the full. Have courage to be who you were born to be, courage to acknowledge your own power and divine connection, courage to steer your own life from your soul's desire and plan.

There should be courage to be human, link and connect with your God in service. Have courage to find peace and contentment in your heart and so understand the purpose of your experience on earth. Have courage for the writer to write, the artist to paint, the musician to play or sing, courage for the carer to nurse the sick and show compassion, for the builder to create.

Life and all it contains requires courage. Many think it takes courage to die for a cause but it takes much more to live and experience, to love and sort out problems with humanity in a cooperation of community.

Great teachers have led with great faith and so seem truly courageous for they have often sacrificed much for their beliefs. It is their courage to have faith which is important. No one has all the answers but to have faith in your life and to have courage to live it is of great importance. Life is full of hardships this we know but above all have the courage to see through the hardship, to achieve the learning to live all of life to the full. The alternative, living life in fear, trying to keep within the lines, without passion for what you do and who you are, is not living to your full potential.

Find your soul, live your soul, live with courage so that when your time to die comes, you know you have truly lived and truly found who you were.

You can take this with you back to your spiritual home and you will have evolved throughout your experience of life on earth.

This is what courage truly is—to have faith in the divine self and your connection to God, to have awareness of this connection and to live it from the soul. The soul plan will be lived out and your courage rewarded in the peace you find in service, service and creation of the life your soul devised in honour of the connection between you and your divine self and God. Courage to be you, therefore, friends, always live with courage.

Positivity

In today's world humanity puts emotional and physical energy into concentrating on the negative traits in life, that which is not going well and that which needs changing. Instead concentrate on the vision of how we would want life to be, life without these situations and perhaps how good life could be and concentrating on the solved situation.

This is a repetitive trait in the human soul; much of this habit is because we have not remembered being taught otherwise. The intellect is designed to mull over and consider a problem, the academic ponders and decides which path is correct or should be put upon a pedestal.

The mind consults, cogitates and delegates, and the solution is weighed up and a course of action pursued, but along the way there may be a fleeting glance of the successful outcome but mind again returns to the problem and the path to solve it or perhaps instead worry about how it will be solved, can it be solved? Drama may ensue and a great cycle of problem, worry, fear, confusion. Despair can follow.

Instead console yourself with the great gift that your God gave you as part of divine presence within each individual on earth, which is the gift of choice, the gift of positive thought followed by faith and conviction in the absolute delivery of the successful outcome.

So the way forward is positivity, the changing of a negative into a positive. Taking what your mind is saying will always be difficult to sort out, so simply be positive. There are many aspects to this, of course. Just thinking, choosing without faith will not bring about your desired result.

This is not just a half-hearted act of "oh well, yes I'll think positive and it will all go away and be alright," No, this is a meaty request, asking more of you than that. It is asking you to believe and have faith in yourself as having a divine spark, part of the divine presence of God in yourself which should be put to work in your everyday life. In the way you think, choose, speak and act in your life for the creation of your life which reveals the true self.

It is this request of you, hopefully by yourself which will deliver you to the solution. For rather than solve one problem to find others appear which need to be solved you will be equipping yourself with tools to see the problem and focus on the positive outcome rather than the problem itself. What we are suggesting here is a final solution which will enable you to look at "problems" in a different way, as opportunities for learning, for clearing and for evolving. To look at them with a different perspective so you can solve all problems with this different approach.

A positive approach which puts you back in the driving seat of you own life. Positive thought is about seeing the problem not as a "problem" but as a situation which has arisen perhaps because of our previous thoughts, for thoughts are things which exist in our mental body and through the process of divine co-creation with God which manifest into reality.

We have free will to choose and what we concentrate our energy on in our mind and mental body manifests when given energy and faith. We put much energy towards our problems and this energy surge then provides a physical reality in the 3rd dimension. It is a process, a gift from God, thought, choice, energy, faith, conviction, creation, reality.

So if we choose to ponder, consort with our energy with all our heart and soul on our problems then these problems and more of the same manifest beautifully into our reality.

Change your thought, choices, spoken word, beliefs, conviction and faith and what is created and manifested in this 3rd dimension will be changed. So positivity can create positive manifestation.

Concentrating on the negative can cause negative, like attracts like, recurring cycles and we know that in the same way positive thoughts attract high energy, negative thoughts attract negative inner dialogue, worry, stress, anxiety which can cause a downward spiral in the body energy as well as in the mental energy.

Negative can be overcome by simple shift in perspective, a thought, a different approach which can release in you a belief pattern rooted in positive dialogue and ultimately in positive divine co-creation.

It is just a thought away. Change negative drama into a new beginning. We cannot stress enough the power you have within yourself to create the life you want to lead. We cannot stress enough also that you are the guru, teacher, healer and co-creator of your own life, co-creating using the God given gifts of thought, faith, and conviction.

You always have choice. One of the obstacles humanity has is that the ego, personality, mind wants to be right. Let us accept there is no right or wrong that is worth limiting your soul purpose for and so the way forward is only a thought away. Humanity can achieve so much and it begins with one thought rooted in positivity that is putting the positive over the negative. Think, have faith in the thought, imagine what the positive outcome looks like, accept it in faith with conviction, it is already on its way. Then leave it in that place and return to it only occasionally boosting it with more positive energy, give thanks for it already being on its way and on arriving. Positivity has power to change your life.

Humanity

Humanity is so much more than it is aware. It has the capability of a different state of consciousness and unlimited possibilities that it has not yet known. It, as a whole, needs to realise and understand that things do not happen to individuals from outside influences but rather human beings are masters of their own creations and so their destiny. There have been many teachers sent to bring knowledge and illumination to the earth and so have tried to teach and reveal the possibilities that are available to each human being. You have been through many eras on earth which have offered much learning and many possibilities. What has not been achieved, though, is humanity learning they have unlimited choices available to them. Spiritual teachers have come to earth to reflect to human beings their own divine and original self. However, instead humanity has put these teachers on pedestals and raised them up higher than human souls and the realisation of self-power, God-self and connection to the divine was missed.

The potential of humanity was misunderstood and all that human beings carry within themselves overlooked. They overlooked the full potential of compassion, love, peace and freedom and of self mastery.

Every human being on this earth is a master of their own reality; it is part of the reason we are here to learn this self mastery and it is taking place every day. This realisation of who we are and what we can do to serve humanity. You have the ability to let go of that which is not working for you and create a new scenario to transform your life.

You are the master of your own life but what happens is the giving away of power to those things outside of yourself, education, medicine and politics are examples of these influences. Popular definitions of success are aligned to possessions and academic success, the job you have or the home you own. These things are important joys for life but it is about the struggle that has been generated to acquire these and what values have been made a priority which has caused dis-heartedness in many humans in the world, competition for these ideals of success have led to feelings of sorrow, stress, anxiety or even once they have been attained joy has been overshadowed by looking outward for something else to give a feeling of contentment. Instead practise looking within in order to achieve these goals of contentment rather than looking for the outward solution. These desires can be achieved without struggle if the power of the human is truly realised and contentment can be found from looking within and finding peace in true self and soul mission ultimately in service by being your true aware and connected unique self within the world.

Comfortable surroundings, things which give you joy and happiness are not to be eluded. The way to it is from a different perspective when the true wealth of humanity is uncovered.

Human souls need to learn about their own power and learn to choose how to keep it with discernment and not give it away to others who determine the success or failure of other souls by the way they look or how much money they have. Rather humanity needs to look beyond and seek true self and power within, to eliminate struggle, to keep power and self-esteem, self-worth.

Teachers come to offer clarity and light and to illuminate humanity to understand the ability and constructs of thought, choice, free will and how thoughts and feelings shape your life.

Humanity has been exposed to many experiences and possibilities of learning and evolution. It is in this time now and particularly when the technology of the future has become so prominent already that human souls have to connect even more to Source, the light within themselves to move forward individually and so evolve as humanity as a whole.

In order for the true value of the technological revolution that is about to surge forward to be appreciated and used in the correct way it is important to first understand the God-self, the divine connection mankind has within. This then can turn into a wonderful communion with science and technology, a new renaissance, one where spiritual conscious awareness meets with science and technology to be of further assistance to humanity.

Souls provide the mission, physical bodies the aptitude of service, mind-science-intellect-technology-the physical tools, come together to heal many problems in the world from the point of true humanity.

First there would be an identification of problem areas, visualising, positive thought, choice, free will, faith and conviction in the solution and technology and science part of the method. No longer either or, but both co-joined. Humanity throughout the eras of its evolution has struggled, battled for knowledge, power, control and has misunderstood its' gifts and so created problems on an individual level but also on a level for humanity itself.

However, today, let us begin today, we can start in this new era to seek, to understand and put in motion all the answers, solutions available to mankind. To create a world of peace, contentment for all, where no competition is needed, where cooperation and the understanding of humanity's true power within, the understanding of the control of thought and choices humanity makes and all it offers to the earth can all be truly recognised and used wisely for the benefit of all of humanity, for it is so loved.

Death/Dying

There is no death in the spiritual body, only in the physical body. The connection we have to it is about choice, we choose the vessel in which we live on earth for the particular learning, work and mastery we want to do in our physical life. We often grieve for our lost youth and energy but we are in a natural cycle where the body ages and is taken to its grave. Many grieve for their loss of vitality but there is an important message not to die before you have finished living and fulfilled your learning, work and mastery.

Continue to live life to the fullest possible, continue to fulfil your soul choices, dust yourself off, spring clean your spirit and continue on through to your physical life's end. Many fear death perhaps for the love of their life but once the physical reality has been lived and purpose of service complete then the only journey left is to return home, to your spiritual home where life continues. Your soul is continuous and takes up the learning of the physical life when it returns to its spiritual home.

Many fear death through the pain they think they will feel. Many fear death because they are concerned whether they will go to heaven or not, dependent upon their belief system.

There should be no fear at all, for any pain in the physical can be tempered by medical advancements in the future and even palliative care is advancing to incorporate a holistic attitude that is mind, body and spirit. Humanity has not yet come to terms with the concept of a beautiful death and dealing with transition of souls from body back to spirit with ease and grace. Fear surrounds the subject of death so much, perhaps because souls are so connected; too connected to physical world. Death is rarely spoken of as part of the transition of life.

The spirit lives on and this communication is one of the many examples of living proof of that. Even if it is hard to comprehend that the soul has chosen a particular life and death then one should at least contemplate the possibility of a good death. A celebration of life whilst you are living, making each day count is a good approach, living with no regret. Each moment counts, living fully in the now, appreciating, accepting, thinking, being aware will allow a new richness of perspective for the life you live and a new appreciation so there can be peace at the moment of death.

In transition back to spirit, a great healing takes place and a feeling of love and warmth surrounds the returning spirit in a welcome like no other. May your death be a good death, may you feel loved, and may you feel you have had purpose and that you have truly been yourself in the service of God.

Death may seem to be a black cloud, darkness upon the life system but it only seems so because of the beliefs held around the passing, the devastation of separation from family and friends. This is why it is important to pave a way during life. Remember to tell people you love them, that you care, that you want the very best for them and you support them in their passions, their dreams, and in their service to God in their particular way. Appreciate life, live it to the full, allow people close and people new to you to see the true you, the one with divine purpose so that if you were looking down at your funeral you would have no regrets. No things you wish you had told people, no things you wish you had done and didn't, no connection you hadn't made.

Make sure in your life you have no regrets, make sure you love your life, yourself and you add value to the world in your own unique way. There is no fear which cannot be overcome; there is no fear which is not diminished by love. Love is the saviour of all and all situations. Death is a transition just as birth was a transition. Many souls leave the earth before their time it seems or in accidents which seem unfair. But know that the souls who have left in this way have chosen to have such an ending long before they came to the earth. It was for a purpose, as all things. This may be extremely hard for us to bear and understand however there is more than the physical experience and learning going on here, there are placements of opportunities agreed between souls. Many souls may experience compassion, empathy and lead to new paths from such an accident and the souls who have gone may well have learned something by offering opportunities to others for learning and experience. A gift.

We are all connected. We are connected by our human experience, by our connection to divine consciousness and by the simple fact we all go through physical birth and physical death. It is in a sense the great leveller despite our beliefs, as we all grieve for loved ones, and we all feel compassion for those losing their lives in an unimaginable way. Again we ask you to focus upon the life in between birth and death and focus upon living it consciously aware of your divine connection. Please see yourself as a spiritual being living in a physical shell interacting with the souls of others, whom you are connected to on a daily basis. It is the soul that counts and it is the soul which continues, leaving behind the body in this life but the soul is the part you have loved with and carried love and will continue to do so always.

Renaissance (Re-birth)

So, we are here today talking of a new Renaissance period. What does this mean? Renaissance, is just a word, meaning a new beginning, a new start, rebirth. So why does humanity need a new start? It is a good question. Humanity can tick along as it has done before and like many individuals who do not change their thoughts or behaviour or beliefs about themselves and then question why they get the same old thing occurring in their life, it is just the same for humanity as a whole.

If humanity wishes, desires, a new hope, a new way forward, a different life, then one must start with self and consciousness to bring about new creations and change in the world as determined by thoughts and change in consciousness as a whole. So what is this new beginning and how can we influence it? Well, it is going on already; it is just a case of learning to be consciously aware of it. Let us perhaps begin by going back to the renaissance of the 15th century. I wish to explain about the difficult times of this era.

It was at first also a time of austerity yet it brought about some of the most beautiful works and advancements in history. Personally speaking, I was proud to have lived in this era and watch the changes happening before my own eyes. I was in the privileged position of being able to have influenced people's questioning and thinking like it had not been done before. There were great intellectual changes and great secrets of ancient times which came to the forefront but it was a dangerous time. It was a time where ego, power and control were prevalent. There was questioning of the power of religion, and corruption was present. The society in which I lived. It was a huge melting pot and lives were in danger because of beliefs held and the company you kept.

It was a little like modern life today but on a raw level. Nonetheless, it was important to consider the path of the soul then as it is now and so this is where the renaissance connection is made. This new innovation period was not talked of at the time. It was something that happened and was looked at later. People started to paint, great artists were born and sent to paint to express the great beauty in life, at the time more for status than for the beauty in itself but the soul of the artist was displayed through his creation. Status was acquired by the beauty you owned. Not particularly a big shift you may think but indeed in those times if the battles became about which artist you employed and how big and beautiful your sculptures were, then this was better and a more pacifying approach to the world than power squabbles which ended in violence. Great music was made and wonderful poetry written. There was study of philosophy and ancient writings, and translations were made so that these texts were made more accessible.

How is this all connected to a new renaissance of spirit to be born today? Well, it is all history, a movement, a shift in consciousness again. Why? Well it is part of evolution, of mankind. We have moved forward in our intellect throughout the ages, technological advancements have created opportunities for all to learn. Computers at first were large cumbersome machines and used by a limited few, now man carries a small device in his pocket and nearly everyone knows how to use them. Man may be reluctant at first but eventually mankind moves forward and evolves. It is inevitable. Then acceptance comes and questioning follows of how we ever managed without the device and we would never question the learning we have undergone to use it. It becomes absorbed as everyday life. This has been the case throughout history. It has been the case for the discoveries of science, the great explorers, the new medical findings, the wars won, the great strategies throughout, the characters and discoverers, creators of the evolution of mankind. Now it is your turn, it is a shift this time in consciousness that is needed, not in physical things in the world.

However, we are here now to help this shift of consciousness be incorporated into the physical world daily. Be absorbed as common everyday life. Individual souls have a soul mission, a purpose, a decision made to add value and evolve their souls, add to the evolution of mankind. So spiritual growth, mastery of who we are in this world and how we can use that in service has been left on the shelf. Technology advances and so has brought about new learning, new opportunities and new purpose for mankind. These technologies can help the sick, the poor, and the disheartened. They can bring a new sense of dignity to those of age and bring back to earth a sense of community and cooperation.

This shift in consciousness is vital for the next stage of technological evolution; this is because technology should be accompanied by heart and soul, these are most important and cannot be left behind. When we as individual human beings understand how global issues are reliant upon group human consciousness and how mind over matter really works then we shall have a new renaissance of learning, of movement in the ways of how people will be healed, kept warm, fed and loved.

We cannot fight this, struggle will not prevail, and fear and judgement will dissipate once we know our own worth, power and ability to create our own world. Life is in our own hands but a new renaissance means a spiritual growth is on its way. A new awareness of our own creative power blessed with scientific advancements coupled with heart and soul from our own spiritual evolution, a new beginning. It begins with each individual raising their own awareness of their living spirit within.

Faith

What is this unseen, non-physical thing called faith? Something you grasp within the thin air, something without substance? Or is faith something acquired through time, through experience, through trial and error or trial and success. Certainly experience, trust in what has gone before and trial and success may add to the possibility of humankind having faith. "Well I saw it work, in action, so I can have faith it will work next time." Is this really faith? It is a type of faith, a faith in the reliance of something, that something will work, but of course this may then let you down when the chips are down.

True faith is the blind unconditional feeling of knowing regardless of proof, the feeling within heart and gut, the knowing beyond doubt. It is this type of faith and conviction that we are referring to when we discuss the creation within your life.

First you have choice of thought, you have your positivity and choice, and then we ask for faith and conviction. Faith in something appearing in your life, rebuffing previous beliefs of not worthiness or belief in failure more than success, we ask for true and complete unconditional faith in what you are choosing to create.

We are asking about feeling it already on its way, being happy it is already here, thanking and showing gratitude for it appearing in your life before it appeared.

The faster the depth of faith is worked upon, the faster things can be created in your life.

The thought process may be different to acquire for some but with practise we can work on the positive thought stage. The faith and conviction has been a stumbling block to many because it means changes need to be made in beliefs and patterns long established. This seems difficult to achieve. Co-creation is a combination of choice, thoughts and faith, the manifestation of the divine spark within. We cannot emphasise this enough that it is vital to work on your faith, the faith that you are able to create new amazing things in your life by using your divine spark.

You are already creating, even though you may not be aware of it. You are doing so with an unfocused power which is going in all directions and mostly focusing on the negative, the faith you have is guided by your environment and social judgements instead of from the depths of your soul with positive purpose.

We are speaking of the new era now to ensure you are aware of what you deep down really know but have forgotten as you have been absorbed by your everyday tasks in the physical part of your life.

In the original era of Renaissance in the history of the 15th century, there were expressions of beauty to stir the soul which were resplendent and forthcoming to assure and stimulate the spark of the soul within each individual.

Today we need to be reminded of the spiritual growth required. The discipline of thoughts and choices and the leap to have faith and conviction in the positive choices you have made. Faith is without doubt. That is it. You must discover for yourself your own strength, power and self-worth to make positive thoughts and then create positive choice and have faith in these. Follow the soul path within you and new opportunities will appear for the universe will offer these to you when you call for them through the process of creation when done in faith.

Now, faith and thought and choice must be in alignment with your true self, your soul, your gut feel. If it feels wrong, you are not yet in alignment. Again faith in your guidance system which God gave you is required, your feelings not your emotions but the feeling of the energy on that particular idea how it really feels to you. Be guided by yourself, not others, take careful guidance, and consider it by all means but it is your choice which is the way forward. Be not guided by what is expected of you but by what you expect of yourself. Have faith in yourself, faith in the God that has offered you the opportunity of life on earth to evolve, to learn and experience and to master your own route through that life. Have faith in your future, faith in your now and faith in your past.

Past, present and future can merge into one in a multi-dimensional lifestyle. One that is difficult for those living on earth in a linear timescale to understand but your faith in the outcome in your future begins with thoughts and choices made now. Many avoid choosing, making positive thought patterns which may not yet show the outcome. The leap of faith feels too far to leap because they fear it may be the wrong way forwards therefore often no choice is made. Just put your hand on your heart or solar plexus whichever feels best for you, quiet your mind ask the question and see what you feel. Life is constantly moving, and with no choice life will either become stagnated and the energy will start to feel stuck. Eventually then the universe and your helpers will try to unstick the energy flow and so situations will come to you where choices will be made for you to move you forward. Often this is by some life changing event. So think, choose and create positively in the direction of your soul path. This may be like no other path that others take but that is because you are a unique soul. We need to have faith that all can move forward along their path to happiness. To encourage and empower others is an almighty gift. To ensure they know who they are, why they are here and how they can move forward is important but ultimately how they choose to follow their path is their responsibility.

When people have had enough of staying still they often move impulsively to something new and seem to act out of character. This can unnerve those who are close by who expect certain patterns of behaviour from that soul, but they are often acting upon their faith knowing deep inside something is not right and sometimes needs a drastic change. Their faith in themselves is working and all they need is to know it is ok to follow their impulses. The rewards are many as they are using their divine gift, the gift of faith. It is an action upon a feeling deep within, a knowing. It is an unquestionable feeling that carries the soul forward to what is right at that time. It is a powerful and important tool we all possess and used wisely and in conjunction with our choice and free will and our thoughts we can weave our way forward to a divine evolution. Therefore, have faith.

Trust

What do we need to trust in as a human being in this experience on the earth plane? Well firstly it should be self. We need to trust in the power we have within us to overcome all of the difficult challenges life throws at us. We need to re-discover our own re SOURCE FULL ness within the contemplation of the era of new renaissance. Trust in God, Source, Creator, Universal force to uphold the framework upon which mankind's power works. We as human kind hold within us the ability to create the reality in our own world.

It is given that God only wants what is best for us, we have free will to choose what we desire within the life plan we have created for ourselves as souls before we come to earth. We have the ability to choose our thoughts, that which we give energy to, faith in and conviction with, be it negative or positive, and it is these thoughts which we relate and suggest to the subconscious mind as the reality we deem we are worthy of and choose to create. Subconscious then starts the act of manifesting it to the physical world. If we so deem God will grant and so the cycle and pattern of behaviour and so our experience of physical reality is ordained. We have used this process unconsciously if you will and ordered via the trusty process of the universe via God's gifts we have been given and given ourselves the life we think we are worth. So, if our life is not up to scratch, if it is not where we think it should be, then we need to change something.

As well we know, no new outcome is derived from the same input. If you want cake you do not follow the recipe for jam. Both sweet but not what the intention was or what we wanted as the outcome, if we follow the jam recipe it may be ok for a while but the craving for cake will still be there and we may feel dissatisfied with the jam after a while just wishing we had cake. Ensure the recipe, the order, the thoughts you use are focussed upon the outcome you really want to order. Do not get diverted or lack focus and let any old recipe be used without thinking. Be consciously aware then have faith, conviction, energy and TRUST.

With faith in the process we have to trust that the input we have given could be askew, we have to feed the universal computer with new data. We have to start trusting we are worth better, trusting in the process to provide and trusting that the outcome will be new if the input is different, a conscious input, an aware input.

How do we start to build this trust in ourselves, this self-esteem, this trust in God's provision of gifts and trust in a new outcome? It is a leap of faith certainly but it is about trust in God and self as co-creating life in reality. Your positive thought or rather your choice of positive thought backed up by attention, energy, and focus in a positive way on that thought, choice plus faith and conviction in the process, that it will give a good outcome. That the process is God given and that God values you all, each and every one. In combination with valuing yourself, worthiness, allowing receiving what you have chosen because God values you and creates with you on the same level which you value yourself. He has ultimate love and care for you and would only desire the best for you BUT it is you that determines what that best is.

It is you who chooses how you are going to value what that best is. It is a partnership because you have free will, a gift from God.

Let us look at the inner dialogue mankind uses on the day-to-day basis. I am scared of doing that. I can't do that. Other people might get that but I'm not that lucky. I can't afford that. I don't deserve that. Who would give that job to me? They are better than me at that. Everything goes wrong for me. Why can't I have that? The simple answer is you can and YOU can give it to yourself. Not somebody outside of yourself, though the process does work in mysterious ways for you may think of something and give it energy... Then out of the blue a friend delivers it to you. No when we say not somebody outside of yourself we just mean you have to go through that process of creation, you do the choosing. You are the key to the process of creation in your life.

If you cannot find love in a relationship then first seek to love yourself and value yourself how you wish to be loved. If you cannot see the way forward in your career then look at the way you are approaching your present job. How does it feel? Is there something new you wish to do, if so, make plans to move in that direction, with learning, volunteering, research, get excited about the possibilities. How would it feel doing that job? Where would it be? Imagine doing the job, creating it and giving it to yourself. Act energetically towards that goal and see what arrives in your life or what contacts suddenly appear.

If you cannot find an appropriate home then decide and focus exactly on what you are looking for with full attention, faith and conviction with a complete picture imagined and focus on that without doubt.

There are many ways we bring doubt into our lives and mistrust in ourselves but none more readily than the inner dialogue we have with ourselves.

It is to be without doubt that we must choose, think, act, to co-create efficiently with complete trust, trust in self, trust in the process of creation, trust in our divine connection with God, trust in ourselves.

To trust that when we become more consciously aware and more consciously involved in the creation of our own lives, then we can achieve what we desire and what we were meant to achieve. It is what our soul working with our suggestions from conscious to subconscious mind and back again, the flow between both, is crying out for, the conscious process not the unaware process.

Our subconscious only works with suggestions given to it. If we suggest something like "nothing ever goes right for me" the subconscious job is to convert that suggestion with focus and energy, so if you repeat it over and over then you are giving full energy to it. If we believe and trust enough in this statement that continues in our inner dialogue and give energy to it then the subconscious does not argue with this suggestion especially delivered with great conviction and of course gets things in motion to deliver via the process of the laws of the universe into reality that which is suggested and behold you receive what you ordered with conviction faith and trust and so situations where "nothing ever goes right for me" will be delivered as ordered by you.

Until a new input for the universal computer (if you like) is given, a new inner dialogue, one that you can give positive energy and conviction with faith and trust that it will be delivered, with a new trust that you with your divine connection are a co-creator of your life and you now change that inner dialogue to "Everything in life is in balance and works well for me for my greatest good" then until this new dialogue, this new input is given, then everything will remain as before.

So be consciously aware of the power of the choice of your thoughts, the power of your choices, the power of word spoken outwardly and inwardly and trust in a process that works, trust in yourself, your worth, your desires and that you can create them. Trust that the choices you make with your thoughts in this process result in your physical reality—just what you ordered for yourself determined by the value you put upon your worth.

Occasionally there will be big clearing events in your life, some perhaps predetermined by your soul before you came to earth for your learning or part of your path, other laws of the universe are at work in this instance but generally the process of creation works as we as have said.

Faith in something new does not always come easy but it is a shift away from the old which we are working towards, working towards a new beginning for all, a new creation with the world and a new way forward for humanity. It starts small. It starts with one thought from you. Now, trust yourself to start a new process in motion. Follow it with faith, conviction, and energy. Follow it with more new input, more new thoughts about yourself, positively, and about your connection to a higher source and the gifts you possess. TRUST.

Word (Spoken)

The power of the spoken word cannot be underestimated. We are always with an opinion and in this day of information offer it wildly but not always with thought and discernment and with conscious awareness. Our choices of words impact others and help to build pictures of themselves. Also it helps them to offer their words and help us build pictures of ourselves through them.

Spoken words have much power and should be chosen wisely. Always with good intention always with a good heart, with love, always with the knowledge and conscious awareness of the power they have for those receiving them and also the impact it will have on those delivering them. The spoken word is a very hefty tool in co-creation.

Jesus, one of our teachers among many, who came to this earth to move humanity forward expressed his teachings with spoken stories, and these spoken words were delivered with Christ Consciousness, conscious awareness of the highest level for the purpose not of preaching that his beliefs were the only way but instead speaking with a new and high energy for the world, with a calm compassion for mankind and a willingness to listen, care and love with his words. His words were healing.

All humankind has access to the same sort of energy; they can choose to speak being consciously aware of the impact of those words. We have at least 50,000 thoughts go through our mind in one day and from those thoughts manifest the spoken word.

Delivered with good intention, good energy and a good heart, these words can change your world, your direction, your relationships and your career. Choose them wisely, speak your truth always. The power of the spoken word is in many teachings and religions, some sing their holy words and some recite but it is the energy the words carry that is important. When they are read, sung with love and not fear they hold great wisdom and great guidance for the congregation listening to them. The vibrations of the words used resound and connect with the emotional body of the human form and so connect and fully transmit the energy of the words. The words must convey a feeling, energy of love and compassion rather than fear, control or condemnation. No one should be motivated by that, instead encourage love, respect, care, cooperation and the feelings of positive motivation.

On a day-to-day level, humanity needs to understand and remember to speak from the heart to each other, to speak what we feel for each other and what we need as well, with honesty, calmly so that we can have open communication for cooperation to develop community. A simple "well done" where it is needed, or a "great that you achieved your goal" spoken with true energy of good will goes a long way to achieving better relationships.

Make intentions to encourage and empower with your words and have no reaction to those things which are negative in energy. The words you speak have come from a thought and have energy attached, a feeling and have been formed in the brain, delivered out loud. The feeling is as important as the word which is chosen. It is unique because it is attached to your individual energy and so even if it is similar to the words of someone else; it has your particular energy added to it. This is where we have to consider always being true self, expressing true self and our divine connection to the world. We are not here to be like anyone else, we are not here to fit in, we are not here to be accepted, we are here to express our individual true selves and connection to divine source, to achieve our souls plan in the form of our true self. Our spoken word is part of that true expression.

Speaking our truth does not mean preaching, expecting agreement, instead it means in faith and trust expressing who we truly are and being accepted for that and in that process enabling others to do the same and respecting that. Above all, bear no harm to others even in spoken word, respect differing experiences and opinions.

Words have power, and they can have great compassion, kindness, and gentleness, but they can also harm intentionally and sometimes unintentionally. In this era of new renaissance, we have to be more consciously aware of the words we speak, of the meaning they portray and the energy they project with them.

That is what this era is all about. In the past we have used words to generate hatred, distrust, to raise and call armies to fight and to use political power for personal gain. This was so in the first renaissance and many other times in history. However, a new renaissance of awareness 500 years later in the evolution of man has seen changes in consciousness. Now we have to act on a daily basis in this consciousness in this era. We have to recognise our inert ability to have power in our own lives and that outside influences no longer need to dictate our direction in life. In this process, we have to be aware of our thoughts, our choices, our words and our energy. We have to take responsibility for them completely and act from our true selves. If this renaissance is begun now, the world as a whole will benefit and humanity will evolve on this wonderful earth into its full potential, its unlimited potential. Words matter, words of love and compassion matter most.

Speak the passion in your hearts, let others know the true you but do it with good faith, good heart and always with kindness, gentleness and love.

Awakening

All that has been given leads to one purpose, it is an awakening of humanity to the strength of their own human souls. The awakening to their own divine connection and of course an awakening to their own power, control over their lives, the challenges to overcome and the power to choose a better thought, make a better choice, create a better life.

It is about an awakening to knowing your spiritual self in the body, vessel, the physical entity, whichever you prefer to call it. Your true self is not the body you chose but that is an important cover to enable you to experience the feelings and emotions and experiences within a physical plane to learn and open up learning for your soul and eventually become a master of you. It is an awakening that you are here for, your soul evolution and mastery of self.

More importantly, you are here to make connections with others on the physical plane. We are all connected spiritually but it is more than that, it is about the realisation of this spiritual connection within the physical life. To co-join the spiritual with the physical, they are already working together, it is how human beings are made but it is the individual realisation of that which is important now, to bring the spiritual, soul power into your everyday life.

It is about an awakening to self, who you really are and where your strengths lie, to fully stand in your own power with truth and justice and respect alongside you. To stand in your full power, your own worth and self-esteem, valued as you are as a magnificent being who can always add value by awakening to the spiritual being you are, having faith and conviction of the thoughts and choices you make. Awakenings which will enable you to move forward in your own lives and in seeing this enables others to seek and find for themselves their own awakening.

We are all connected, the awakening to self brings the joy in life and peace and contentment in life from inside out. Seek not the outside for peace, instead awaken to it and project it out of your being. This reveals the inner energy to others and so can affect their perspective and they can go on to seek their own way to peace and contentment. The term "awakening" is not some out of reach spiritual term only achieved by those that have studied for years in philosophy or the ways of the spiritual teachings it is already there inside of you and the awakening is simply realising who you are, how our souls are connected to our mind and body and the purpose of this connection.

The mysteries of the world, writings from ancient times, books re-written, esoteric, philosophical, spiritual and religious texts all have value. They have hidden truths and much has been disguised and with good reason. To protect those in keeping of the texts and to protect humanity until it was ready to explore and truly understand. In the past much was misunderstood and misused, power was held by those with great ego and certain truths in their hands at that time would have caused an escalation towards further misunderstanding.

So now with advancements in technology and science in general and a move away from the doctrines of religion, an evolution in intellect of humanity it is time for an opening of the mind and heart, an exploration for purpose and a new beginning in seeing what is important in life in the physical plane.

Humanity has for centuries sought to find answers to the mysteries yet has really overlooked the answer to the most unresolved mystery, the mystery of the human soul and its connection to the divine. We are in an era of awakening to the way we can approach life in a new way. We can no longer retreat into finding solace in the things we surround ourselves with.

To have beautiful surroundings and the joy of a new car or things for your family is not denied, we are not to all be living in a sanctimonious poverty. No, we are not saying that we have to be poor to know ourselves or abundant either, after all, we have all encountered the duality of life and its opposites and experienced them many times, and we have over many lives lived well in wealth but also in poverty and sickness, health and much more. It is part of the physical experience. It is much more than that, your soul is bigger than that which is in your body and its desires and so has acquired much learning over many lives, all at different rates, at different levels, all our choice to evolve our own souls, our healing, to help others in their evolution and healing too.

Now we have to step up, not sit back; we have to seek in another place. We have to take responsibility for our own lives, our own choices, we have to step into our own power and at the same time connect to the divine spirit within us which reveals love, compassion for all the aspirations of others. Enable them, encourage them and help them to seek within themselves and create from a point of cooperation and community. This is not a way of levelling all humanity to the same level; it is a re-awakening of that which has been forgotten. An awakening to just how we can create and what we can create when we work together at our own personal level in awakening our spirits to who we truly are. To appreciate uniqueness, diversity and create a community where all reach their unlimited potential in a way which brings about a true renaissance, an evolution of human spirit and an awakening of self.

Balance

Life needs balance, particularly the balance between the spiritual and the physical, between the mind, the body and the spirit. Balance between work and rest. Relaxation is not something you simply slip in where you can; it should be a determined part of your schedule. Relaxation is not to be underestimated for it is a time for you to connect to your inner self, to check your inner dialogue and so help to connect with who you truly are.

It is where you can collect the day's interactions, to present them to yourself, to enable you to see the lessons from them, to sort out that which worked for you and that which was no longer useful. We should do this on a daily basis. We should retreat and form opinions of how we managed the day, the targets we set and what we achieved and more importantly what we achieved from our true self perspective.

Let us wonder how much could be achieved with more relaxation and reflection in balance with thought, choice, words and action. Balance in the universe is important and so it is for each individual in the day. Some good intentions, good thoughts, good choices, good actions help to keep the balance. Balance in food and exercise to keep our bodies and our minds healthy.

Tremendous health can be established with a balance of all these components, making decisions and choosing the right path at the right time.

Look at the way nature balances itself in the different seasons, time to spring forth with new energy, time to be full and fruitful, time to harvest what has been sown and take stock and time to hibernate through winter and emerge once again refreshed and new to start the cycle again. It is a lifetime cycle which has worked since the beginning. It is a natural cycle and humanity often forgets that this natural balance in all things is a necessary part of us for we are a part of nature. We not only need balance between our mind body and spirit but also between us and our environment. We need to recharge our batteries but also those of the earth. We must keep a balance between that which we use and that which we replenish.

There is always enough. There is no need to fight over oil, land and food. This is born out of fear and greed, we hoard supplies, protect the price of supplies and affect markets and incur huge wastage, partly due to fear of not enough but also because of keeping the price high to achieve wealth. Countries even go to war to protect the supplies they have. Yet many teachers have come to the earth to teach us to have faith that the universe, Source, our God will always provide and many miracles have been performed to reveal the abundance which comes with faith.

With true love for fellow man and not working from a position of fear of loss or not enough a balance can be achieved for all. With absolute faith and knowing, the balance of abundance to all and for all is a relevant and achievable goal.

Love conquers all and enables all. We can achieve a balance in our lives, with our relationships and with the way we treat our bodies and our earth home. We are connected to this balance of nature; we are whether we like it or not part, of the nature of the earth.

Without this natural rhythm of the stars, planets, moon and seasons we are lost, yet we have the contemplation of these things and the attention to our body and spirit connection way down on our priority list.

So take the time to balance your life. Include in it time to spend with those you love, those who inspire and empower you, those who support you in your passions. Make sure you make time for those passions, for the things your soul has come to experience. Make sure that the light within you shines. Make sure you choose balance, take time for the right food and exercise, for learning new things, for fulfilling your purpose and carrying out your unique gifts.

Take time to live in the now, not the past for the past has gone, remember the good things and bring them forward into a present experience but do not dwell on that which has already been and no longer serves you. Yet *keep balanced in the now* and be not tempted to move into the future too far for then you may miss the present and so many alternatives in the future linked with the present experience. The future is made from the past and present decisions, from the choices made and the NOW is an important balanced part of the process.

Balance in all things for only with a balanced life can you achieve the mind, body, spirit connection of this new era. The power of you is with you, in you, we all have a divine spark and so there has to be balance for you to be able to access the true energy and power of you as a unique individual in the picture of the whole universe.

Whenever you feel out of sorts, it is often that your energy centres are out of balance. You are not aligned with your true self, and thus you are not in balance. The main seven chakras, energy centres, are attached to various energy bodies which make up your aura. Some centres may be running too fast others too slow. There is much information concerning these centres and it is important to be aware of them.

We as humans in this busy world can be easily put out of balance and it is our responsibility individually to put the balance back into our lives continually with rest, work, food, thought, exercise, care of the body, mind and soul all in balance whichever way this works for each individual as long as it is part of their conscious choice.

Balance brings with it peace, health and well-being. So try to find your own individual balance.

Soul

Without soul we do not exist. We are mind, body *and* soul. We are immortal beings with souls who are connected and have been over a period of lifetimes, and soul is why we are here. Sole purpose is soul evolution and why we experience life on earth, to experience each other's souls in a physical experience and also to appreciate the connection of the spiritual with the physical parts of our being. Why then do we feel so disconnected from our purpose? Why do we go without rhyme or reason down a pathway not knowing where it is going?

Soul knows where it is going. Mind may disagree but even the avenues taken away from the soul path will lead to learning, learning about what is not right for us and help to find the unique path we are to tread.

These journeys may not seem to be in any particular direction sometimes. We feel we are drifting but it is part of our purpose to connect to our soul who is leading the way within us.

In this conviction a greater understanding and alignment to that which we are meant to achieve. We often feel astray, a lost ship, this indicates we are not aligned with soul and an indication that perhaps we are off course.

When you are in alignment with your soul plan, there is a knowing, a feeling that all is well, a gut feeling, an instant, an inevitability. Following this instinct is not always easy but it is a matter of faith, faith in yourself, your choices and being responsible for them but also to constantly connect with your soul to revise, re-plan and realign. Your soul is in charge, you, the personality, and the ego self has to align and understand this, struggle, battle of ego vs soul ends up in more challenges and often a feeling of separateness.

Our souls are even greater than the part which lives within our body in this life on earth, and the body is only part of who we are. We fear our true light and power because our reason, our conscious mind does not fully comprehend the extent of the universe, its laws and just how great and diverse and unique we all are on this earth, yet all the same.

We were given gifts to use when our soul chose our life on earth; we came with everything we need. The soul has life experience, learns and takes back with it the knowledge it has gained. It continues to return to earth many times and if you can imagine lives many imprints of its own whole. The whole soul does not come to earth for each life but lives as many personalities in many lives, experiencing and learning and evolving and raising its consciousness and in turn everyone helps raise the consciousness of humanity.

We are not the most evolved of souls but we are working on it and as we all become more consciously aware in our living of our day to day lives and how we live with and love our fellow humans on the earth, then humanity as a whole raises its consciousness, both its mortal and immortal consciousness.

The soul that is here on earth in this lifetime, an imprint, a part of the whole higher self, if you will, is only part of the whole of you, it is still connected to the greater and higher self which has learned through many lives and on this occasion in this life has brought with it some of its learning from previous lives, also some of its challenges to overcome that were not dealt with in previous lives and a selection, if you will, of gifts that are needed for this lifetime's goals.

The soul is the essence of you and records and carries with it, all experience on earth it has lived through and with this knowledge evolves in spirit, back home, using all that it has felt, experienced and enacted upon earth. Therefore, it is important to be in touch and aware of your soul and its connection to higher self and ultimately to Source. In being aware of your soul connection to your life experience and the challenges tackled and overcome in this life you become more aware of your soul's role and who you truly are.

Being in this awareness provides a way forward when processing your learning on return to spirit. We are all living spirit in a physical body, living souls. Soul is not just formed when we experience death and returning to spirit form then. We are living spirit in the form of soul connected to higher self and Source whilst we are in the physical body. When the physical body dies soul returns with all it has experienced and is received with love, healing and a great welcome. Then learning and evolution of soul continues on the other side of life, in spirit. Perhaps after a time a choice to return once more to life on the physical plane on earth may be made or to experience life in other parts of the universe or indeed to remain in spirit to help others on earth sometimes in the form of guides and helpers when ready, for many purposes then, for we are multidimensional beings.

The message then for now is to follow your passions; live, laugh and love from your soul and so allow yourself to align with your soul purpose and so be consciously aware of your true self and your real purpose for being here. It is to enjoy life, to spread joy, to raise your own consciousness and enable your soul to grow and evolve here on earth and beyond once you return home. Allow then your soul to evolve into the best your soul can be.

Education

Education encompasses of course a great deal more than what you learn in school or from books or other learning instruments. Life experience is part of our education. Life experience enables us to learn from our emotional body how experiences in life feel, it is of course the way forward to be more in touch with these feelings that new experiences offer us.

We should, however not discard academic learning, reading, and writing and in the new technological times listening and typing. How humanity acquires information has changed and so must the way humanity absorbs this information. We have had discussion, debate, consideration and discernment when we learned from old texts and books, the written word. More so these times when you are bombarded with information it is very important that this debate, consideration and discernment are still achieved.

The choices you make determine your belief system and from that point give you, each unique individual, a point of reference which in turn determines how your conscious mind makes choices and gives suggestion to your subconscious which in turn with faith and conviction set by your belief system creates your manifestations in your reality.

So discernment within your information received as part of your education is paramount.

So learning is considered lifelong. Formal education starts you in a direction, helps you find perhaps for some people where your gifts lie. Many do not sit well with that type of schooling but this does not mean they cannot be educated. There may be many reasons why it doesn't work a particular way. Perhaps your gifts lie in an area which is not taught in school. Perhaps you have a wonderful unique creative gift that has never been seen before and you are bringing that to the world.

Maybe your brain patterns work differently and settling down to the formal way of learning restricts your creative learning.

There are many reasons but no excuses to stop exploring other learning in different ways outside of school. School is one place, a long experience, but school is school within a school. For all our lives on this earth are learning within the school of earthly experience for all our souls. It is a great experience and much can be learned. Discernment is needed. Once the bearer of these messages was told she was not academic. She now has a degree and a folder of certificates, diplomas and is now helping to write a book to pass on messages from ancient times to the new era of learning and acceptance. If you accept what is told about you by others you will sit at that level of energy. If you take on that role you will become what they believe you to be. You will limit yourself through your own thoughts and choice of accepting what they have said.

But if you decide and choose that is not who you are and break free and move forward in faith that you can become who you want to be, express faith in yourself then you can succeed and will be given the help required. Then through example you may serve as inspiration to those who have little faith in themselves, so pass this on. *Receive with discernment that label which is put upon you, consider whether it is your truth, then choose your way and allow the same in others.*

There are some in your world of the physical plane who have come learning differently and these are often referred to as learning with difficulty. We are adamant that all can learn, all can add value; they have gifts and ways of learning in different dimensions to that of the traditional learning. They receive and offer information in a different way to people who learn with traditional methods. To adapt to these traditional methods takes great energy in them. They often lose self-esteem and self-worth in the process of education and the system needs revising. Testing and qualifications will change to a system where self-esteem and self-worth can be kept intact and in this way new teaching methods will be required.

We must look forward in this era about taking responsibility for our learning and continue to learn our lessons and appreciate the learning. We have many gifted souls on the earth who are troubled and have not found their special value. This is very important that all know that they can achieve their goal, each soul has a gift, a purpose, and it may be to help others in their learning. For to be able to teach those who learn differently, some souls have to volunteer to be those who do learn differently. That is their gift, their adding value to the world, they offer the opportunity for some to learn how to teach in this different way but mainly they offer an opportunity for others to learn about uniqueness and how creative we are as humanity.

They offer us an opportunity to see that the boundaries and limitations we set are just that and that those that learn differently may indeed be higher in the realm of learning than the accepted boundaries but just different.

Education then is more than what is or isn't learned in school, it is gathering of life experience and academic learning and other learning beyond any limitations. Real education is a progression which keeps the self-esteem and self-worth intact, enables growth of spirit as well as the intellect and allows learning from others and the passing on of that learning to enable and empower others to be their full unlimited selves.

Happiness

Happiness is very individual, of course, and we subconsciously strive for happiness within our lives and often seek it out in places where we cannot really achieve it, perhaps a temporary feeling but this then subsides. It is perhaps because we look in the wrong place or perhaps we strive too hard or even we strive for something we feel will bring us happiness and yet when it arrives, it does not. This may be because we have been influenced by outside elements, which determine this or that will make us happy. When in fact, it is inner peace we seek. We seek what makes us calm, peaceful and stable and secure without fear, and it is this which leaves us with a feeling of true happiness.

How is this achieved? Many things acquired can help to this feeling of stability or security but if it is someone else's choice then it cannot truly satisfy us. Happiness is individual, which is true for the reason of choice. Soul choice is what will make us truly at peace with ourselves. A contentment which is brought about by aligning with our own choice, with our own belief system, with our own soul so that we can be our own true self, in our relationships with others in our careers and our choices within our family and our home.

When we can derive this peace and contentment we can feel happy within ourselves whenever we go through our daily lives, instead of just living from one happy moment when we have bought something until the next happy moment some time away.

There is happiness in every day. The Buddhist way offers a system for learning how to achieve this but it is one of many paths to release suffering and to be consciously happy in our everyday lives. Their way is a system of belief that suffering is caused by want/desire and if we stop wanting and look inward for contentment through daily practise of meditation then we can find a pathway to peace and contentment. However, whilst this offers reason and method, once again, we can only emphasise for you that the choice is always yours. The choice, thoughts of what will make you happy is often simplifying your life and working towards a simple life and goal. Your own spiritual philosophy, if you will, for your own life.

In these days many decide financial security will make them happy, often when other issues come along, perhaps with health, we see that money becomes a secondary issue.

Life has its way of changing priorities. We can always make adjustments to our choices and we can decide what level of abundance will serve us for our soul level to complete our mission and allow us the happiness, peace and contentment we wish for.

Our happiness in this way is in our own hands, and it is our responsibility and of course it is always our choice.

Outside influences are not the guide of our lives and the target for our happiness. Many instances have been written about when people are facing their supposed darkest times find happiness in the smallest of things, perhaps being able to see the flowers opening in spring, the song of a bird in the garden and the joy on a child's face eating their first ice cream.

Life is full of joys; we have to choose to see them, hear them, and speak of them. Again our choice of thought, our choice of perspective, our decision in spite of the outside influences and challenges that life has offered to us so far, is to find the positive aspects of life and go forward with faith and conviction that more positives will enter our lives.

Seeing the positive, accepting the challenges and having faith they too will pass and not attaching to them means that the peace and contentment within can settle and see you through even the most limiting challenges. Always take the lesson, what you have learned from this experience, whether it is a challenge or a blessing or both and then be thankful and grateful. Then move on with peace in your heart and faith that all will be well, all is well and all has always been well.

Happiness then is a choice, a state of mind, a place in the heart and a suggestion in your subconscious. Life can be happy if you seek it within. Simple things, life choices, thoughts which bring about change, love of self and determination to have positive perspective, faith, and connection to the divine spark within you will all bring you to that place where happiness can be sought.

Everyone on earth has experienced challenges in many forms, some challenges to one person, is another's blessing, after all, life is unique and diverse, and it offers you what you choose. Your happiness is simply dependent upon one thing: YOU.

Knowledge

Knowledge of the mind, intellect is an important part of the whole entity that we are as human beings. Knowledge has to be in context of relativity. What we think we know for sure often changes in the future, it evolves. People once believed the earth was flat until knowledge of the world was revolutionised by exploration.

This new era is an exploration of self and a review of the knowledge we have and know to be true. It is ever evolving, revising with new discoveries and it is up to us to evolve with it, use discernment always and choose our new standpoint. Knowledge like ourselves does not stand still and so we have to have open minds to review and revise our individual and communal belief systems.

What is known to be true is not necessarily all of the knowledge. We do not know what we do not know yet and when new knowledge whether it in science or religion or spiritual genre comes along we have to see it in its broad perspective. New knowledge may indeed broaden the whole aspect of the previous knowledge. Often discoveries are made which no longer hold the previous knowledge to be true but we must not throw the baby out with the bathwater as you say for part of the original knowledge may indeed be relevant still but just not fully understood in the context of the new knowledge at that particular point in time. Often new perspectives are revealed when humanity has evolved to receive them.

What this means really is that we should always question and learn and evolve and regard knowledge not as a finite thing but instead something that evolves always, ever engaging and adding new parts to or replacing existing knowledge. We are explorers of this knowledge in all realms but most of all we must be explorers of our own knowledge of ourselves.

We as human beings are much more than we understand, we are not just physical beings. We have a consciousness, a soul which has purpose. The soul is our immortal self and lives on after physical death of the body. It acquires feelings and knowledge of itself through its life experiences. The body, the shell, is our choice for the purpose of acquiring this particular knowledge and experience. What makes you, *you*, is the soul within and the knowledge the soul acquires is through the many feelings from the challenges and blessings felt throughout life on earth.

Knowledge in this way, for the soul is an accumulation of feelings experienced, not academic knowledge necessarily though learning in this way also evolves the soul, the lifestyle and emotional experience together covering mind, body and spirit together evolves the soul and fulfils life purpose.

If we live our everyday life and forget to explore within ourselves, who we truly are, then we are only experiencing part of the experience of knowledge. The intellect is a huge part of life on earth and all leave with more knowledge than they came with. However, if we fail to look a little deeper at the term knowledge we miss out on a deeper progression and uplifting which is available to us in the human experience on earth.

We are looking at knowledge here in a broader aspect and in terms of connection to who we truly are, why we are here and how when we are consciously aware of these two things we can step forward with this knowledge and create for ourselves and our fellow humans a world which has considerably more blessings than challenges.

We can see that if we step into this knowledge about ourselves we can step forward in a different way in the world. We can achieve the peace and contentment we desire within and so bring a new value to the world. We have to make choices in life and discern about the information which comes to us in all forms. We have to keep re-establishing our centre point and balance again just what we believe in. It is a simple process and much information which comes to us so quickly these days has to be discarded but some has to be considered and discerned, questioned and decided, in relevance to you, your soul, who you are, does it serve you and your true purpose?

To acquire knowledge without this discernment and repeat it without it being YOUR truth means you will be misaligned to your truth and purpose. Consider your own thoughts, choose, discern, then stand in your truth peacefully and add value from your individual, unique standpoint. Add value to the world with your considered knowledge. Then you can be aligned with your own soul purpose and work from your soul and be consciously aware of doing this within your own everyday life. This will bring about a new beginning for you as an individual and in turn the new era, a new renaissance of cooperation, concern, community and compassion. Discernment is the way forward to make best use of just what you know.

Friendship

One of life's joys is the friendships we make, the friendships we keep and the new friendships which are yet to be. The connection with another soul on the same level, the connection with another soul who is very different yet complements.

The friendship which provides us with opportunities to help and be helped is an important and integral part of our soul learning.

Before we come to the earth we are part of a group within our spirit world, same soul energy, agreements are made, sometimes for many lives, to help each other on the path. These are our long-lasting friendships and sometimes even family which help us through our challenges and celebrate our blessings. Today, we must remember to appreciate and hold those friendships close, as we are souls in a physical world, and we are in need of these interactions with other souls. It is part of the human experience but it is at the same time part of the soul experience, and part of you evolves on a different level within these relationships. Often human life offers real trouble, real difficulty and real challenge. These often manifest in difficulties within our relationships.

That is the hard part of being human dealing on a daily basis with hurt, pain, loss, grief because you have loved.

Your soul cannot help loving. It is its natural state but we often lose our way in life and so we feel fear or that we are hard done by.

On occasion we feel some sort of betrayal, injustice, because we have trusted and loved. These times are our greatest opportunities, for as we have said before we are in an era where we are to become consciously aware of how we deal with creations which appear in our reality. So we can accept, rise above, focus on the peaceful resolved situation, heal, offer healing and in doing so move on in forgiveness, then acknowledge the lesson and evolve into the solution. Enable growth on both sides and sometimes learn when the time to let go has come about.

Sometimes friendships are for a fleeting moment and people change and move along. If this happens then send them with love, keep the good times in your heart and wish them well. You will be reunited one day perhaps not until you return home in spirit and return to your natural state of love and respect for each other. Be grateful and thankful for the challenge they offered you, the opportunity for learning they offered you and the growth which has occurred for both of you.

Of course, some friendships stand all challenges and blessings with ease and grace and you stand side by side through all. That is meant to be and a wonderfully rewarding experience for both. Give great thanks for that; it is priceless. Remember in the world of spirit there is no monetary cost. Money is an energy exchange and there are greater abundances on earth than monetary wealth.

We choose our experience we are to have on the earth. We have all experienced the duality of life both wealth and poverty. Without life experience we do not know what it is we desire to learn further and which experience is suited to our soul purpose.

Let us get back to friendships. It is a fine line sometimes between love and hate, the duality of life. In life we can often compare what our friend has or is doing in life. It is this which can bring about the negative expressions between soul interactions but this is not soul based, it is from the physical interaction, the ego, the mind and personality.

Real friendship is seeing the true person inside and loving that person, helping them be the best they can be. This is the charge of a true friend. Goals of unlimited potential are easy to support for the true friend. It works both ways, my friends. What you give out is what you receive and so we have to give from the heart, open the heart and interact on a true soul level.

We are easily hurt as humans. We are much more sensitive than we would openly acknowledge, the ego, the personality provides an outer shell which can keep the pride intact, which can cover up fear, which keeps true self locked away. Yet if we have the courage to live in conscious awareness then we can really start to achieve more true friendships, more bonds which encourage and enable natural state of love to ripple throughout the earth.

Friendship, love, courage to be that which we truly are, is close at hand. The courage to step into conscious awareness of the fact we are souls, here on earth to learn, add value, encourage, empower, teach and reveal to others who they are and release their unlimited potential and innate state of love to add more value to this wonderful earth.

It is an ongoing cycle born out of love for humanity from Source, God, Creator. The divine spark of co-creation through love and friendship within us all is what is going to be achieved in this next era, in this golden renaissance. Remember how beautiful those friendships are, how valuable. Take time to nurture them, my dear friends, and value the friendship of humanity, and make earth your friend too. Friendship then is a divine gift, one we should all receive and one we should all give.

Respect

Respect is needed in all things. Simply, without it there is no trust and without trust we cannot build faith, without faith we cannot co-create. It is an important fact of who we are that we not only respect our fellow humans and their different and unique belief systems but also respect ourselves enough to value others opinions and respect and love ourselves enough that we can be our true selves.

Respect is a complex fact-of-life and without it, relationships are hollow. We need to know and respect other people's truth if we are to expect the same from them. It is a mutual connection. It is not I'll respect you if you respect me; it is not a conditional practice.

To begin with we need to respect the fact that we ourselves need to respect who we are and why we are here, when we respect ourselves without ego, personality, arrogance and come from a centred and balanced standpoint then we find it of no consequence what others think of us instead we go forward with self-worth and self-esteem to add value to the world. This respect for others becomes part of how we live in the world; it is not something we need to work on. We see in others what we feel in ourselves. We feel the need to be respected for who we are and we see the same need in others.

Connections, we need not agree with their opinions and their beliefs but we can respect the fact that is where they are at this point in time. Belief systems are continuously evolving, people change and their choices change, so others rarely stay still either as they too evolve in life.

There are some who may argue that some very old traditional religious beliefs do not change. This may be so but what happens is the world changes around them. It moves forward and learns and evolves into something new and those that strive to keep everything the same in a changing world often create struggle and challenge as change is a natural force and law which is inevitable. So with change interpretations on traditional doctrine may offer new perspectives, the values held within may or may not now be still appropriate to the changing world but it may indeed offer a basis for a new doctrine based on core beliefs and offer a more appropriate base for a changing world. In this way, old doctrine and new perspectives can merge and be respected.

There is a way therefore to maintain the essence of traditional belief and the new core beliefs of the modern world. It means looking at those core issues and what they are actually trying to teach. Respect and love are components within many old teachings and these are still valuable today. Change is inevitable. It does not mean letting go of faithful beliefs, of love of family, respect of your God and duty to your community. These are wonderful and valuable goals in life but we need to adapt the way we offer these to the world and respect those others who may not offer their beliefs in the world in the same way as us.

We can respect these core beliefs whilst not agreeing with the doctrine which upholds them: the practices which can limit people.

We can respect the need for these at a certain point in time but in adapting how we live our beliefs can enlighten people to the core issues instead of alienating. Often religious doctrine offers limitations, boundaries, but in a changing world we need to look at the essence of all religions and focus on what unites these. In amongst all religions are teachings based on love of family, respect for fellow man, respect and love of your God (whichever faith you have or if you have no faith respect of that). It is all to do with your relationship of love, faith and respect.

It is about connections for good. It is about respect of others views without trying to convert them or admonish them for thinking and believing differently. It is about allowing people to be who they are. Respect is a divine gift, we choose whether to respect someone but if we respect ourselves, hold ourselves in our truth without ego and without transforming others but merely respecting their rights to have a peaceful truth about who they are, then there is no harm in having a wonderfully rich tapestry of diversity.

In some ways it is all one, for we are all souls connected to each other and these differences are all pathways to the same enrichment of your soul. They are just different pathways. We learn from differences perhaps more than from those who share the same views as us. If you look at the essence, the essence is love.

When belief is strained and so respect is difficult then this is often due to fear not love. People fear change for many reasons: they fear they will lose their power; they fear they will not survive; they fear traditions upheld and valued for generations will vanish and they fear for their stability and security.

Yet, if their faith was restored away from fear and re-connected to the love essence of their particular faith, relationship with their God, many of these troubles and fears would dissipate.

Many follow many different faiths in peace and co-exist in mutual respect. Those that find this difficult are connected to fear. It is this they must address and in the meantime we must respect where they are at that point in time and instead move forward in our own essence of love and respect, for love defeats negative patterns of fear, always.

We must stand in our truth and be who we are meant to be in this world, be who we truly are, step into our true power, not one through the pattern of fear but instead in our divine connection to God, directly in our essence of love and use this power of love, respect and faith for the benefit of mankind.

Respect is an important facet of the love for humanity. It is perhaps one of the most difficult to establish, to seek out, it gives us great challenge because we have to look deep within and question our own beliefs but if we go to the root, the essence of who we truly are, if we look at what we want to achieve in the world we see that we have to connect with this mutual respect.

Often it is tied to forgiveness; it is tied to our own values of self-esteem, self-worth and our own beliefs in what is right and what is wrong. Our souls have experienced all sides of life in many lives and so developed many different perspectives and in doing so learned to respect all from their perspective, the soul has learned this. We forget in our daily human life to re-connect to this knowledge our soul holds and the essence of love for all that is carried within us. Now it is time to respect on this soul level to love and respect. It is time to remember, feel and express this love and respect.

Hope

Hope is a positive step on the way to faith. Without hope, in a situation with challenge, sometimes an individual cannot find their faith. Hope is a more positive thought it is a wish for a positive outcome. It is a desire towards the positive; it is not yet backed by faith and conviction, important parts of co-creation, which in turn is a pre cursor to a shift in higher level energy in the creation process.

The positive cycle of co-creation is stirred by a positive thought, which is energy in progress, in alignment with choice and soul purpose, followed by the faith and conviction that what you need is already there for you, already on its way. Your level of energy when this faith and conviction is truly at the level needed will rise to the level required to be in receipt of what you have put in motion. It is a natural state of co-creation using the power of your positive energy.

Hope is not quite the faith and conviction stage but if you are in a deep challenge and you can have a feeling of hope then you are on your way forward to a positive creation. You have the stepping stone of hope. It is a move towards something more than the negative cycle of thoughts spiralling downwards taking your energy and the potential level of co-creation with it.

Without hope as a stepping stone towards the process of putting your power in action, many would be stuck in a negative spiral; however, we do not want you to stay in a continuous state of hope, we would wish you to move forward to a deeper faith that you are in control of your life with the use of the gifts given by God, Source, Creator. Faith is important, complete faith is better still. We are talking about a knowing in the heart that all is well. This takes courage to abandon the fear which has continued to form in your life, in the form of challenges which test all of your beliefs. That is why challenge is there, to ensure you understand the processes of the universal laws in place.

Challenge comes for many reasons but you have a part to play in this process and your mental attitude, your choice of thoughts, what you focus upon, makes the difference to how quickly this is solved and moved on.

Hope, "I hope this will be better tomorrow" or "I have hope that he will get better" is a positive but not as positive as " I have faith he will be well" and that is not as strong as "He will be well" or "He is already well" and with faith and conviction, belief, knowing in your heart. They are all levels and it is a learning to get to those different levels of hope and faith.

Hope is a part on the way there, it is an improvement on no belief in something better, and it is a wonderful way to faith. Without hope humanity may be lost, as a step or leap into faith may be hard but once humanity learns to live consciously and in faith of who they are, and how they create in the world then they can heal and repair their own lives and others too. Then we can begin to see that hope plays only a part until we understand more about our full power and the process we go through to create.

When we truly understand in total faith and go forward with conviction then we no longer need hope, for we understand. We think, we choose a positive outcome or particular route in life in balance and alignment with our soul plan. We jump straight to faith, knowing it will be manifested as we have requested, it cannot be otherwise as long as we have excluded doubt in our thoughts and choices.

Hope allows a little doubt. It exudes a feeling of "I have some faith but not quite enough to sit fully in it." It is on the way to faith but not quite there; it offers a desire to some outside force which will make sure that everything will be alright. So, it gives away some responsibility and power. However, we do not desire to make out hope is not a route to be chosen for it is along the way a rising up of energy and should be considered as such. It however should also be realised that from a position of hope work still has to be done to stand fully in your power and steer yourself to faith. Faith is the place where you know it is all well and whatever you choose in positive intention with heart, soul, full faith, energy and conviction will be delivered into your life.

Hoping it will be so IS a step in the right direction but we are asking for you to leap, fly even, in the direction of your own wisdom, faith and power. This will mean you have full control of your life, you have the responsibility for your choices and thoughts and actions so if you are standing in your full power of who you are then your need for hope will be diminished.

It is a stepping stone for those who are on their way to finding their full power and becoming consciously aware. It isn't meant as a permanent position or even a temporary cure. It is an uplifting on the way to something more wonderful than at the time could be comprehended.

Once hope is in place it enables a higher energy to serve you and carry you on to faith. It is more than a stretcher, a first aid kit, a plaster; it is a wonderful and exciting move forward. It is a step in the right direction; it is not the final destination. We are creatures who focus on the negative, the drama, so readily that we need hope to lift us up towards a place of imagination of the best in this world and the next. We must use hope wisely and still focus on faith. Hope however holds us ready for faith.

Cooperation

Humanity needs cooperation. There is much competition with each other at the moment so division results in this busy world. We have forgotten an important part of being human is to work in cooperation together for common goals. These common goals include our own spiritual advancement and a learning of being consciously aware and then onto mastery of who we are.

It is a simple shift of conscious thought to help others be their highest self. In this, we can also receive learning how to be our highest self. When we help others we feel good about ourselves, there is a little voice that says that was good, it raises our own vibrational energy and allows us to promote who we are and release our energy into the community in the form of our true self. For a fleeting moment when we react to help someone out, we are revealing our true soul self especially when it comes from instant action without pre-meditated thought.

This cooperation between others within families, friends, and individual communities then moves further into wider areas. We cannot continue in a world where competition leads the way, in this we miss many purposes of life. Business has competition and that is necessary to some point but we can have that with cooperation. How we run the business, for the intention is important, for the greater good, adding value with integrity and good spirit for the working community. There are many who put money first and this is a realistic aim to run business to make money to keep your family well fed, housed, educated and well looked after.

However, we must look at ways to incorporate in this a cooperation with workforce, a cooperation with your clients from a point of view of adding value and this in turn will bring about a realisation that we can achieve more than a good profit margin, instead this can be achieved and business can have soul.

Life is about the interaction, interaction between others and between various situations the life experience offers us within our life span. If you can achieve this added value within humanity, within your business goals then its success will take care of itself.

If you see this business as a service, whatever the business is and an expression of your true self, of your passions and of your gifts then you are on the right track. If you cannot generate this feeling of passion and of great cooperation with your customers then revise, review and find your way to a better business plan.

Cooperation is now needed throughout life and is not restricted to just business but can be centred on our friendships and relationships in family. It is about what we can add. Life is for learning, the most wonderful learning is captured in our relationships, seeing what others need and how we can help them with that, giving service is the essence of our being and also giving a service to our spiritual selves too, for we are here to learn spiritual lessons also. We learn most about ourselves in our interactions and connections with others.

Tomorrow is another day, and in our linear lives from yesterday to tomorrow, we seek to be happy and contented and secure. We do not realise that the true security is in the love and respect we can have for each other in working for each other. Rejoice in the success of your neighbour rather than envy him and what happens then is that you will receive others rejoicing in your success. In giving we ultimately receive—not just in kind but also the feeling we have in giving itself. Cooperation then is a deepening respect and love for your fellow man reflected in the thoughts, words you speak and actions you have towards them.

There is much in the world we do not understand, when we go deeper, when we take the time to know the people we judge too quickly, and then we find that we have more in common than we thought.

We are all in this life together; to learn to be the best we can be, to find out about our own spiritual self. We are all facing life's challenges and life's blessings we are all learning about our strengths and our weaknesses and we all are here to help one another through, we are all connected, we are all one family and it is through these life experiences we become our true selves, we become able to help others to become their true selves too. Life can be hard and it is in these hard times those with true faith must help those who have not yet found their true strength to their path to conscious awareness of just who they truly are.

Life needs each other, life needs us to cooperate in the physical reality as we do in the spiritual life.

Life can be joyous then through the hardest of times. Life can be led to hope and a light can shine through to guide the disheartened. The joy of cooperation, caring, compassion is seeing someone else strive, beat the challenge in faith and rise to their unlimited potential. To serve another soul is a wonderful honour and this honour is bestowed on all of us to use. To cooperate with our fellow man (even if they make it hard sometimes) is a wonderful honour we must remember to teach cooperation on all levels to the future guardians of the earth, the next generations, that is, if they don't know it already for the next generation have come to fulfil this in the world.

Community

Community holds within it the word commune, to be as one, we are all connected, and we are all one, though the physical reality may not always reflect that which is true in spirit. Sometimes the challenge of physical reality is indeed seeing beyond what seems to be so. We as humanity are a community and we share many commonalities, many common goals, and many shared experiences. However there are also many instances when the physical reality challenges us, where we see disruption, war, disillusionment. We cannot always see the community of the world as one but we CAN start from the centre of us.

We build relationships, friendships, and join with partners. From that springs families, schools, churches, temples, synagogues and communities. These communities often reveal our uniqueness, our diversities and sometimes these differences can instigate that which isn't community, setting the differences upon a pedestal and concentrating on the differences instead of the feel of community, it can divide and separate.

True community of course is seeing these differences just as they are, beautiful uniqueness, co-creation at its best, diversity is not the enemy of community instead it should be welcomed as part of the world community. These individual communities should be part of creating a wider world community which reveals to us the wonder of diversity but also the template for more communities to be built. That common ground between humans that can be shared, the wealth of knowledge, the joy of learning, the shared passion for animals, it takes little to start a community. It is a living thing which grows beyond the reason it began, new friendships hold fast, a feeling of belonging and a wider reach to other people beyond the normal interaction.

Community spirit is acting together for the greater good of the people within it and outside of it. We are all connected through the journey of our souls, through life which brings us a common ground, we are all connected in that we are born, have a soul and continue to work our way forward through life's blessings and challenges, we die and our soul, greater for the experience, returns home in spirit form to enrich others and review its progress and learning. This is the common ground to all humanity whether your beliefs are one way or another, how you live within that journey is your choice, and so it is.

We can deem to make the journey adding value, or we can choose not. The achievements, direction, intention of each soul is indeed up to that soul and not for anyone else to decide but the idea of world community has a certain ring to it for we are all in it together. We are all suffering challenges on one level and receiving blessings on another. Life is never all bad or all good; there is duality present in life. The experience is in knowing both and learning to be able to shift and see the good within the bad.

Community offers two things in this. Firstly it offers us opportunity to give and serve and add value and support it and secondly it gives opportunity to receive support, knowledge, wisdom, guidance, love, compassion when this is needed. We need to restore community feel and build it strong from true and faithful foundations and in this supported extended family we can become our true selves, stop the false competition, reveal our true concerns and receive true support and encouragement.

Without community, life would be hard to bear, the challenges harder, the blessings shared within community are greater. The ancients knew the value of the divine bond of community. It has an (unknown) invisible strength which otherwise would not be experienced. It is a unique bond between many unique and diverse human beings.

There are many areas in need of a community on earth. Many areas in need of love, in need of care to find the common bond but there are many eager to start this work and think it needs money or something outside of itself to begin.

Yet all it needs is a calling together of people with positive intention and love in their hearts, an open mind and a pooling of all the divine and diverse gifts they have. Youngsters can come together with a ball, a project in making a community garden which could help feed those with less to eat, a group to make cakes for birthdays and use the recipes from the wiser and elder members of the area, a group to write down the memories of the older citizens to promote the history of the working communities. There are as many ideas as diverse gifts and unique individuals, pooling resources to make it work. Just a little goes a long way, there are millions of these gestures performed every day throughout the world, they are done from a point of love and respect because one soul identifies with the other in love and respect and so sees the need, offers the solution, makes the bond and the cup of tea, for all is solved with a cup of tea; millions of gestures, marvellous, gorgeous gestures, actions of love, intentions, all over the world, within communities. We need more of these, for in serving, adding value for others we stop seeking for that which will make us happy and content outside of ourselves and instead we see that it was within us all the time, the feeling, the knowing that we are all connected and can help each other through life on earth.

We all have something to offer, a smile, a kind word, a moment, a walk with someone, a cheery joke, a glass of wine, a shared meal, the options are endless. The thought, the intention, starts a pattern, a co-creation with your HIGHEST SELF in conjunction with your HIGHEST BEING (God, Source, Creator) whatever you name them within your own belief system, working together in communion for the purpose of the bond of community. Love and respect are the deep emotions held within our hearts. We need to move in the direction of our hearts to enable the sense of world community to endure. This message is an important one for your time now and is sent with deep love and blessings for your community always.

Responsibility

Many dislike this word "responsibility" and what it means. It is, my friends, unavoidable within the journey of human experience on which you embark. It is true that shifting of responsibility (so called blame) is rife within the world at this time. Blame is simply placing responsibility of the act or situation onto someone. This could well be the correct person or it may well not be. Judgement is in this action and we have to look at this very carefully.

It is true within a society that laws must be upheld, that is also true in the universe as a whole; there are natural laws of time, relativity, gravity and many yet to be understood and discovered. All these naturally govern the way things work and interact in the universe. There are laws which are man-made within different societies.

Usually when we are looking at responsibility we are looking at situations when something has gone wrong or astray within the boundaries of that law. We often call upon justice and punishment. These may be relevant to each individual case; we must, however, ensure that truth prevails.

We must allow for an act of responsibility on both sides, the responsibility of the soul which has perpetrated the act to be truthful with themselves and be responsible for that act. Perhaps to forgive themselves and seek that which ensures the action never re-occurs.

The people involved who had the unjust act thrown upon them have also a responsibility to their souls to seek the right outcome to ensure they do not live in resentment but let go of bitterness and move forward whatever way they can in their time. These are huge requests and it involves forgiveness, truth, patience, love and compassion rather than blame, bitterness and resentment. However, why we ask this is because all souls ARE responsible for the thoughts, choices, actions, behaviours they carry out in life.

Many blame outside influences, people or situations as to why these acts occurred or place it at the door of what they did not have or the love they did not receive. This is a hard challenge to start in life without the right support but that soul has chosen it for a reason and here there is a bigger picture. For some souls offer themselves to experience and act out that which is not good, some because they are offering opportunity for other souls to learn and also for their own souls to experience the duality of life, others because they have not felt the high energy level of love and so perhaps perform acts on a lower level.

Please do not judge these souls within the immediate situation alone, as there may be a bigger picture here. However, there is always responsibility here, to be understood by the individual soul, this will be dealt with by that soul here on earth AND when they review their life choices and lessons and challenges when they return home to spirit. Forgiveness cannot occur if there is nothing to forgive and forgiveness is one of the great lessons taught throughout all religions and belief systems throughout the life of mankind.

If we learn to forgive and receive forgiveness and let our own souls free we have also learned the lesson of responsibility to our own souls and the choices our souls have made.

We must also look at the responsibility to our families to be our true selves and to teach them this individual responsibility to their own souls, the thoughts they have, the choices they make and their actions and co-creations have consequences they are responsible for. If this is taught so that they are always in line with their true self and that right thought enables right action we can see that the difficult business of punishment and blame cannot be a factor in our lives. We are only responsible for our own choices and actions. It is all learning, one which is not easy for mankind, as humanity has so many facets, so many choices of behaviour and many reactions of emotions in many situations.

We create our own lives, and we are responsible for our anger, our behaviour, our thoughts, our love and compassion and our creations in life and for our own self-control. Others may interact and we search for reasons why we couldn't achieve our goals but we need to be aware they are just challenges sent to us as creations we have chosen to rise above, to make us stronger and carry on to learn about our passions and goals and to attain them whatever comes to us in life. Not to sit back and give away our power and responsibility to others.

Some situations may be grave, serious, deeply hurtful and challenging and we are not minimising these at all for the soul that goes through these challenges are wonderful gentle souls who need love and compassion and support, but beyond that, they must learn that they have the ability to turn these challenges around and so the first step is to be responsible for the life you have now, in this moment, and deem to change it if it needs changing for the better. To move forward in the direction of the new, the different, a higher level of energy with love and compassion to self, taking the responsibility to give that love and compassion to self first and then to others.

It is the same for all souls, no matter what the challenge life brings, there is always a way forward, once we take up the responsible mantle we can move forward, first in intention then in thought, choice and action bringing to us the higher level of energy and with it the opportunity to make life a little better for ourselves and others.

Sometimes the lesson is to act unjustly and receive the consequences. Sometimes it is the act of forgiveness we must learn. Within this complex web of responsibility we must first move towards being in line with our true selves, accepting that we are in the driving seat of our physical life and ultimately we are responsible for our choices and actions.

This may weigh heavy on some souls but it is a part of the learning of life and it is perhaps the greatest of lessons, for we are responsible to our own souls first, then our family and friends and this can then broaden to groups and communities and then humanity as a whole.

With this responsibility comes a great freedom, one which enables you to set your spirit free within the realms of your own justice and integrity and love and compassion for your fellow man.

It is a personal responsibility first and then a collective one. A responsibility to make positive changes, embrace positive thought, develop positive faith and deliver a positive outcome to the world in your own unique way. You are in charge as individuals; you are always responsible for you. A responsibility only YOU can have to treasure.

Forgiveness

Forgiveness is a subject which arouses much concern in this world and on earth. Here we see it as a part of your own soul's healing, in essence there is nothing to forgive for there is no judgement directly as we consider no right, no wrong. It is all experience and we would not advocate violence and any other hurtful occurrence because in an ideal world we would want souls to work out their difficulties in a peaceful manner and so when we say there is no right or wrong we come from a spiritual perspective, from a place where there is only love and connection to all and healing from the experience of the earthly life and challenges faced.

We realise that in the physical reality things happen to those we have loved and even to self which are difficult to overcome. It is here at this point we would remind you that you are a spiritual being learning from experience in a physical body and some of that learning incorporates that which needs forgiveness. When we say from a spiritual perspective there is no right or wrong, we simply mean there is no judgement here from others, there is only self-review and self-forgiveness, healing, love and compassion for those souls distraught about the pain they may have caused in their lives.

The only judgement would be by the soul when they review the life on earth they have lived and so there may be within the soul the experience of regret, remorse and the need for understanding. Healing is offered to all here, for those souls who would want to learn from that experience and so they will review their actions, the consequences, the responsibility and the healing. How does this help the souls on earth left behind with the consequences of an action they did not expect and which has left them devastated and desolate or in despair? Well that is a challenge too and learning and healing is sent to them when help is asked for. Sometimes this has been a joint agreement made prior to their life beginning on earth; the bigger picture is a bigger learning and soul experience than we can comprehend from a physical entity on earth point of view.

The help and healing on earth comes in the form of forgiveness. This is not about condoning the act necessarily, or even forgetting it, but it is about, over the course of time and within the soul's own choice, accepting what has happened, choosing not to let it affect the rest of the life on earth and allowing forgiveness to be a part of the experience, letting it be closed and enabling movement forwards.

In written word this seems like a simple act and we know only too well that this is not. For it is one of the biggest challenges in life to accept hurt and move forwards. We know from our own life experience and we do not ask other soul's to consider this lightly but it does come from a point of love for the souls on earth that we ask this. For we cannot bear to see those souls so stuck and hurt. You must designate a time when what has been done needs to be released. The soul cannot move on to sole purpose with anguish and pain in their heart. Love for self enables this process, support is often needed in this from friends, family, loved ones and/or professionals guiding the soul back to love and light and if this is not possible on earth, there will be healing, and it will be done when they return to spirit.

Yet, when this happens, this healing would be better done on earth for on return they would remember the agreements made, the opportunity of learning offered and some may have wished to place forgiveness in their hearts sooner.

We are all in this together and part of the new spiritual renaissance is teaching, my dear friends, that the very biggest challenges in life often offer the greatest learning, the greatest rewards to the soul.

In learning the process of forgiveness one can offer this to others on earth, in service, add value to your life and help others too. What a gift to come out of such desolation. It is an opening of the heart, to release that which has caused anguish and pain and to turn it into compassion, empathy and understanding and practical help for souls who have gone through similar despair.

Forgiveness may also be needed on a simple level for an unkind word or a false accusation, but again we need to remember to stand in our truth, the truth in our hearts. We are human and so often react without thought. We react in fear or anger, which is fear disguised, and we ask that time is taken to renew thought and action and forgive those who have not yet understood careful awareness of thought and choice of action. Forgiveness may be of a small act or a greater one, but the process is the same, an opening of heart and releasing of your connection to an emotion which will be limiting and imprisoning for your soul in your physical reality.

Therefore, it is a cleansing, freeing and healing act to practise forgiveness of the small things and the large and remember that within the bigger picture in doing this your soul will be filled with healing light and love and so be free.

Consciousness

Consciousness is the stepladder to a more content habitation of the earthly challenge. When we align our consciousness to our soul purpose and connect our physical being to our spiritual being, we are then truly becoming more of who we really are. It is apparent that we are moving into an era that is one where we are to be more consciously aware in the way we live.

Beyond this life we are spirit. *We have come to this earth to learn many things but mostly about who we are.* To express our spiritual being in our physical being and also through our physical being enhance our spiritual being, raise our consciousness through the partnership of the spiritual and the physical. Many discussions about what consciousness is and why it is important have occurred throughout the ages; many discussions with many viewpoints for consciousness has many parts. We have a conscious mind in the physical form which carries out our everyday decisions. We have a subconscious mind which is predominantly reactive to suggestion and soul connected.

Consciousness itself is about raising our energy, our vibration, our frequency. It is not so much an intellectual mind raising up, instead it is a raising up of vibration, an understanding of feeling, knowing who you are, as a spiritual being and seeing your physical life in a different perspective because of your spiritual understanding.

It is not really following meditations, therapies and an increasing of your academic knowledge or knowledge of spiritual philosophies, although all of this helps raise vibration and your understanding.

Really we just need to understand our connection to God (again read here whichever Highest being suits for your belief system, we honour all) but your connection and with the highest energy and knowing that power within you to make your individual world better and the world around you too. Consciousness is not something for some and not others. It is indelibly linked to all of us because we cannot avoid having a level of consciousness for we are all spiritual beings. Raising our consciousness though really is a matter of choice, a choice to be open to something which is greater than us, to connect with it and to live with it every day.

People often struggle with this concept of raising their vibration. Why should we bother? We are spiritual beings and opening to a higher vibration helps us to glide along and above the challenges we are sent. This does not mean we do not experience them without feeling, ignore them, bury our heads and float over them. No, this is different. It is accepting them, seeing them for what they are and that means seeing the opportunity in the challenge, accepting and forming a perspective of a higher consciousness, vibration, a higher knowing if you like "that this too shall pass" moving forward and raising above it in a non-attached higher consciousness perspective.

A higher consciousness enables a new perspective on life. We can raise ourselves up to achieve the best outcome. More importantly, we can raise ourselves up to the truth that we are more than our physical selves and that our physical lives have more purpose that the reality that they seem to offer every day. It is about a greater understanding, an understanding of where life really fits, an unconscious understanding, consciousness is about knowing, and in that knowing having a feeling which is greater than you feel in your physical life, a higher understanding, not a higher intellect or academic knowledge though this is a great attribute. It is an awareness of who you are in the context of the universe and a connection to that which is the highest Source, a connection to Creator, God and serving on earth in this consciousness.

We are from consciousness; we are greater than our ego and physical being. We are quite magnificent beings. We are spiritual beings born of consciousness itself. There is no beginning and no end just a series of experiences born out of consciousness and energy transformed. That is what our experience on earth is about, transforming the energy of our souls. We are energy, and this energy can never die but it can be transformed, raised up. We as human souls have transformed, we have stepped out of innocence and moved forward, now we have to move forward further to see we are capable of higher consciousness and that through our life experience we can evolve.

Once we appreciate this perspective we can see we are all connected and in our connected journeys together we transform our energy. If we become aware of who we really are and how this transformation works and for what purpose, we can bring a new perspective of a higher consciousness to the world and become aware of where we really fit into the world. Having a higher conscious awareness of how we all belong and living life from this connected centre point means that we can learn in a new way and more importantly serve in a conscious way.

There is no class which reveals what this higher consciousness is, instead it is gained and gathered up through self-exploration, a gift in itself, a knowing, a getting to know how you create, how you are in power of your own life and an ambassador for service in your own unique experience of life, your own unique consciously aware experience of life. Therefore, each of us brings uniqueness to consciousness itself and a new contribution and so consciousness itself evolves and you are a part of that creation.

Compassion

We truly are a compassionate people, we have no other way of being, in our hearts, and we cannot be anything else as souls on earth, yet we forget our hearts and our souls and allow our mind and ego to take over. Occasionally a disaster or worldwide problem steers us back to our hearts and we feel for our fellow man and this brings us back to our heart centre.

Life on earth is born out of the spiritual but we forget this and live day-to-day from our physical perspective from our physical point of view. Now is the time for us to incorporate more the perspective of the heart. We have great compassion when these events occur but often we resume our normal lives and get frustrated and irritated in our day to day interactions.

Compassion for others is a necessary part of humanity's evolution and there are many souls on this earth who live from this point of view. We have to have a compassionate heart full of understanding. Life is full of opportunities for us to demonstrate this. Most of all we need compassion for ourselves. For the love for self is not selfish, that point of view belongs to the personality and not to the spiritual self. No, we need compassion for self to learn self-love and from this strong standpoint we can begin to see the connection between us all and so then put into practise compassion for others.

Compassion and love and respect are our natural spiritual state. We have plenty of opportunity. It is our choice whether we take this opportunity up. Compassion and love for your fellow man brings about its own rewards. *It is unlikely that when you show some compassion in the smallest way that you cannot feel some reward yourself.* This is not to say we should do compassionate and charitable acts for the reward. That will bring a different result to you as the intention is different to that from the natural heart centre.

True compassion is empathy, is love, is consideration and needs no reward. Love has its own rewards. Life lived with love and compassion is a life of peace and contentment which brings about its own rewards. Every day in your life choose a compassionate and loving path, for you can find in that path, self-love, self-knowledge and a knowing of a higher consciousness, ability for you to be your highest self. These opportunities are all around, it takes no time, and large charitable gestures are not necessarily required, though these are also appreciated. There is no ego involved here. We just need to see what is needed, give a little time and many tiny gestures, make a difference to self and the others you give to, time to talk to those who need an ear, to exchange ideas, to offer help and to connect with your fellow man.

In offering help for those in trouble, your own troubles are often diminished. The focus of worry and helplessness moves from your own position to helping, to solving someone else's troubles and so a new thought,

201

a new choice, therefore a new perspective has been offered and in so doing you have shifted your energy. This releases and raises up your own vibration which in turn can bring you wonderful opportunities.

Compassion is a wonderful interaction, one from heart to heart, soul to soul. Souls have nothing but compassion and love for each other in spirit. Souls are still learning in the earth plane and offer opportunity for us to offer our natural state of love and compassion. However, we must also learn to receive this compassion. If the intention is one of great love, then receive the love, open your hearts to connect and receive that which other souls offer you, which too opens up and raises your vibration, your energy.

Love is a great thing, for all the days we have on this earth should be filled with love and compassion. These are the greatest gifts we can give and receive. If our hearts and minds work together, then we can bring about change in our world so quickly with ease and grace and feel so much better about our learning. The raising up of our energy to a higher level will instigate a spiritual awareness with a world working from a positive mental attitude and a warm compassionate soul, a new earth, a new beginning, a new spiritual renaissance.

Compassion is seeing the small opportunity and offering from the heart for God's grace has given you the opportunity.

We have no need of fear that this small gesture will not be enough, a feeling that more needs to be done; this may be so, but doing nothing means the results won't change. Doing something, however small, filling your day with many small gestures offers you an evolution too, a rewarding contentment within your hearts.

Compassion is a wonderful gift from God, one undervalued in our world, and sometimes we miss the opportunity and instead we turn to anger, blame and a call for justice; however, we have other gifts to offer. These are simply respect, love and compassion.

Truth

Truth is matter of perspective because you have, as a soul, to stand in your truth. What is true for you is a matter of choice, a matter of thought, belief, environment and as we have said before a matter of your connection with your own soul and purpose. It is too easy to be waived by popular thought without discernment but the truth by which your soul acts and aligns its purpose within its connection to Source, Creator energy is what counts.

Now in standing in your truth and operating from that position, we are not suggesting that you impose that truth upon another soul, for there must be mutual respect too of that soul's truth. How the interaction then moves forward between you is a matter of choice, love and respect. Respect of someone else's perspective because their experience may have been very different from yours and so it is an opportunity for a learning of different truths within one lifetime and so we need to look at this prospect.

There are many opportunities to see a new truth, a new way forward. However, it must be said that one truth is not necessarily above another. It is about perspective you see and a unique perspective. There are some truths in the past where they have been said to be immovable, only to find that today a new truth has been added which has overridden the former truth. This has moved forward and evolved energy, thoughts and truths change because perceptions and humanity changes and evolves. *Truth then is not an immovable object.*

It is a perspective set in a moment of time from a unique perspective, a unique soul and so we must understand that we need flexibility in our outlook, an openness which enables our truth also to shift.

At each particular moment in time we should stand in our particular truth and honour our soul's perspective and purpose, be true to our true selves but we should not be rigid in perspective as this can change in a blink of an eye. Truth throughout history can be different from many angles and so much is discussed and believed about what has gone before. It is perhaps best to understand that truth in the now is important and then truth in the next moment. To speak your truth has much to do with your understanding and experience of the now situation and also has much to do with the intention behind your truth. To speak from your soul with love, respect and integrity is a good intention to understand that those receiving your truth ALWAYS have the choice of whether to receive it or not, and this is an important part of this consideration. I have understood many truths from many perspectives in many lives, but often the complex context of these truths has been overlooked.

There is often a bigger picture which has not been seen and so truth is subjective, objective and contextual. We understand our truth from our point of view in that moment and often when we have more information sometimes from another perspective, then the picture changes and we see truth, our truth differently and sometimes others' truth too.

If we operate from an intention of integrity of our soul truth, from our hearts as well as our minds then we have spoken, thought and acted from a real truth. However, if our truth is to win over another, to convince to determine or control someone's choice, to take away their responsibility then our truth falls short. We need to realise there is equality in truth. In our truth we cannot speak of another's truth as mightier or lesser than ours, it is different; it is truth part of unique self, our personality self which is part of our whole self. It is a vibration from which our core works and so reveals part of our self which cannot be anything other than part of us. If we offer a truth which has been swayed by others without discernment then we are not in OUR truth. We are in someone else's truth and handing over our power, our responsibility and creativity to someone else, this does not mean we cannot agree with someone else's truth but if we do and we have used discernment then it is our truth too.

It is about not just accepting what others say without exploration, for we are here to explore, learn, experience, to discern who we are and who our true selves really are and part of this is then to go forward in our unique expression of our own unique truth, whether it be accepted or not.

Now within this there are laws of universe and we must abide by them but we need to observe, question, love and respect those offering their unique expression of their truth and in this is a wonderful expression and honouring of the diversity of humanity. Without this diversity, evolution would be very slow, without discussion, discernment of another perspective and point of view, offered in unique expression by different souls we could not find new truths, view ideas, new beliefs and so the world would become a stagnant place without change and move forward very slowly.

Truth is important within every day human interactions but it has a deeper purpose; it is an expression of unique souls. True self needs expression and self-truths are part of that. What do you believe? Why do you believe it? What else is there? How can it be observed from a different perspective? What is your soul truth and how do you express it within your human existence every day? Truth is not one thing; it is many things to many people and this diversity, these different perspectives offer opportunities to humanity to be open minded and express uniquely their unlimited potential. Therefore, your neighbour's truth may not be yours but it is as important to humanity and its evolution.

Religion

There is a need in this new era to review religion in a different perspective. Before we begin this review it must be determined that we are coming from a perspective of honouring all belief systems within all religions and without. We honour humanity's choice, the individual soul choice and this review is merely an offering for a different perspective in order to help the individual souls to be more consciously aware of how they live in the human experience.

This is not from a point of judgement, there is none, but from a point of helping discernment, of helping souls to see who they truly are and to release any limiting beliefs and rejoice in those which help them to raise their vibration. This is different for all souls. This now said let us explore a religious review.

Religion has played a magnificent part in the structure and framework of societies which has enabled mankind to reach for something outside of themselves, something beyond the day to day survival targets and goals of food, shelter, and warmth. To look beyond the physical self and explore a spiritual connection to God, Creator, all that is whichever faith people belong to.

In context of ancient times this also set a pattern of laws, boundaries of behaviour, which in turn became rules, a doctrine of behaviour for followers of a particular religion. Throughout the ages religious texts have been offered and received and these have been relevant within the context of the time in which they were written.

Many may have been lost and many texts still may be uncovered which may bring new meaning to existing texts. Within the boundaries of time religion has had its place for it has delivered wonderful structure and exploration. It has also sadly, often due to misunderstanding or misinterpretation of the true context of original teachings, lead to war, pain and separation between mankind.

In the spiritual context we are expressing here, we are observing it is time for a new resonance of spirit with your particular God and this is really expressing the divine in a different way. Life is full of challenge and so what we are advocating is a unique expression of connection with the highest being of your individual faith. The choice is yours, as it is your neighbours, and so we are saying it is for your soul to choose to connect individually and uniquely and directly with Source, God without religion as it is known, without the formality of boundaries and limitations. If you will, we are advocating a simplification of the process of the spiritual exploration a soul makes and the resulting connection to God. We feel often, much of the connection is lost between a man and his God via the ritual and more determination is needed, not in a system of reward and punishment, of the worthy few against the less worthy but more concentration via soul work to really connect, to be consciously aware of one's own ability and that with cooperation one can seek and find God in order to create the life you came to achieve. In service of the God you have faith in.

Now, religion and its doctrine do not have to be cast aside in this, we are advocating a shift in perspective of it. If all religions were viewed as an equal pathway to a divine communication and connection so strong with your God, then you as an individual would operate from a standpoint of strength in your connection and so go about your business every day in that strong connection standpoint. The same respect would be honoured for your neighbour and so all the unique souls on earth. In this way there would be no need to fight over which way life should be lived, the choice of each individual's right to a connection to God would be observed and honoured and whatever route, pathway, religion, they chose to do this, would be up to them. Individually to explore, individually to practise as the human right would be in the individual's connection directly with Source, God, and Creator.

The teachings of other doctrine itself could be explored if so desired but not necessary as needed in the past. In the past different teachers walked upon the earth, teaching different methods, which offered different religious pathways, there were many more religions which did not survive not the few we now have on offer but of course many of these perspectives are not seen today.

Religion is partly manmade, the teachings sacred in all religions, some misinterpretations along the way but individual souls have choice in this; they have responsibility too of exploration, discovery and discernment. So in the past there was a need for preaching to the masses, as many could not read many teachings were spoken and passed down from generation to generation and in so kept from being lost and honoured above other teachings. So let us remind ourselves here all teachings are sacred, all souls have choice and discernment and responsibility. These days souls can explore their spiritual lives with much more ease due to technological advancements and information.

However, religion is not just texts sacred though they are. It is not about ritual, though sacred this may also be, it is not about sacred space, temples, churches, and mosques though sacred they are too. We must not forget the important purpose of the connection of individual souls to God expressing that connection of love and bringing it to the world in their own unique way. This can be done whatever faith you have. Therefore religion in this world today needs a shift, a shift in perspective of upholding an individual's connection to their God through the pathway they choose, all pathways have equality.

In this within the religion itself a shift of perspective to allow all individuals that equal right. The power then and responsibility for each soul's spiritual journey, experience on the physical plane is put back in the hands of the individual and the everyday action they carry out in their faith and so too is the individual relationship with God and the responsibility within that relationship.

Fear

There are two roots for all actions. They are: love and fear. We often do not realise when we act in fear for it is hidden under many other reasons, excuses and emotions which give us a supposed defined reason for inaction or action.

Fear is a limiting belief pattern, often not one justified, just a pattern learned, perhaps over many lifetimes. It holds us back, and we justify we cannot do something because it is not the right time, or we do not have a certain skill, many of these things can be overcome and if we analyse the repeating patterns of our belief system we can follow to the root of fear of failure or even fear of success. We fear jealousy of others, of not being liked, of being pushed away, of being held apart as something separate, of not belonging. We fear we will not be loved unless we achieve *a, b or c*.

There are many forms of this very basic root emotion. It is the dark part of our soul. It is connected to self-love; we really need to look at why we do not love ourselves enough and to embrace the dark part of ourselves, the part of us that feels weak and fearful. This part of ourselves is as important as that which is strong and skilful. We are all a combination of strengths and weaknesses and in this exploration of life on earth we are to find out about all the parts of us. All of us, the things we fear often reveal more to us than that which we love about ourselves. Nothing is one or the other, for earth experience is made of duality.

When we embrace that which we fear, we just simply acknowledge it, accept it is there and move forwards through it, because we are more than our fears. Once we love that part of ourselves we need not fear the fear itself and so there will be a release of the limitations attached to it.

Many actions in our lives are achieved from fear. Controlling behaviour can be a fear of change, being alone or similar emotions. If we are stuck in a situation it may be fear of the unknown, it may be fear of not being secure.

To explore the fear on a deeper level requires courage but is often worthwhile. We can question ourselves as to what may happen if the worst of the fears come about. Often that which we imagine is worse than any scenario which would play out. It is here that courage of heart is required for it is to be joined with your own thought power. Many of these fears are within your thoughts. As has been mentioned before, thoughts are energy. They are things which can create form in your lives. Focus on fearful situations and imaginings of the worst outcome becomes a habit, courage to change this pattern is needed, courage and awareness. So change the thought, and focus on what can be done and how that feels, raise the vibration and change the pattern of fearful thought.

When it is realised actions can come from fear or love, it will be a great revelation that focussing on what you love, what can be done, the positive, a thought from the point of self-love, all of you will achieve a better result in your life. Love conquers all, it conquers all fear. Surround your inner-self with love, love yourself fully, think positive and focus on the positive.

Fear is limiting, and it disguises itself as anger and violence and war and this is rife in mankind in the earthly experience. Fear of change, death, evolution. Some of these are born out of a lack of understanding of the way life on earth really works, on what reality is and how you can live from a different perspective. Being consciously aware of the true self being a spiritual entity with divine connection, with power of co-creation, in a physical being, enables mankind to dissolve the fear of that which it clings to in misunderstanding.

Man fears death, but there is no death only the decay of the physical body. Man clings to the physical because the personality self thinks that the physical shell is who we are. We have attachment to the body when we fear we should lose it in death. The answer then is, love the body you are in now and enjoy it whilst you are in it. You have chosen it as your garment of choice for this life, so love it, all of it, care for it, maintain its good health, respect it, until at the end of its life you bid it farewell knowing you have truly loved and cared for it but know also it is only a part of who you are. It was what you thought of as your garment of choice and so co-created it before you came to the earthly plane in love for its purpose.

The soul or part soul which resides in this body is you also, the immortal part of you, the core you, the true self, and so there is no death to fear.

Being consciously aware of this allows a release of fear and an abundance of love in the now for the cooperation between body, mind and soul in what is your life on earth now. Fear of what will be happening in the future will take away appreciation of now and therefore limits your experience. If you fear death because you do not wish to be on your bed of release of the body with regret for things not done, things not spoken and not shared, then simply love your life now, fully, as it is and release these fears by doing, loving, speaking, and sharing. Love conquers all; be motivated by love not fear.

Mind

Mind is complex; we are intellectual beings as well as spiritual. We are body in physical realm, we are soul dressed in a physical garment and we are mind that bridges the two.

We have conscious mind which enables us to work and survive and live in the physical realm. We have consciousness to question our own being, its purpose and search for that which is higher than ourselves. We have subconscious which is a mysterious part of ourselves which acts upon suggestions fed to it by conscious thought and is a part of the creation process, which brings thoughts to form in the physical plane.

It is the combination of all of these together which brings about a complete experience within the earthly experience.

Intellect, academic learning is important for some souls, it may be soul choice for the purpose of their spiritual goal in this lifetime. For others the academic learning is not as important this time as perhaps the creative, art, music, sculpture, working in fields, or with bricks building the creative aspect of life. All is valuable in this life and all will be remembered by the soul energy throughout the many experiences a soul lives through.

Mind enables us to sense and perceive from the senses, it is if you will, the input part of the whole, along with the processing unit, the brain, subconscious mind is open to suggestions perceived, focussed upon and so sets to its task of delivering thought into form. It is aided by soul in its purpose it has come to this life for. It is conscious communication between soul, mind and body which brings about co-creation and that which is desired by the soul in true service.

Mind alone will often bring struggle for it is concerned with the physical, the logical, the personality, the ego self. Spirit/soul alone would not be able to contend with the physical world and would lack the bridge between the body and soul. Body would be needed for the physical enactment of experiences. The soul and mind could not experience without a vehicle to carry out acts within physical reality. Body on its own would be a mere shell. So you can see how all three together make a good team.

Mind can get carried away with itself for it takes in and perceives information from many different sources within the physical reality on earth, particularly in the new technological era.

It convinces itself of many situations, uses outside influences to back up beliefs about self and so is often reliant upon personality, ego, self, to form a picture of self. It protects this picture and derides any attack that the picture is incorrect.

Soul however knows better it has a knowing of itself that it is more than the physical being within which it is clothed. Mind can play tricks on perception of self and so self-esteem; self-love and conscious self-knowledge can be lost. We are more than the physical and mind has its purpose but it has forgotten its role as a bridge between soul, body and itself. It strives to stay in the physical reality and denies the divine spark of the spiritual within its body.

So, the conflict of beliefs and struggles within the personality self begins. Mind controls conscious thought. We have thousands upon thousands of thoughts per day and so where these thoughts take us leads to the reality of the life we experience. If mind convinces us and focuses on the negative, it builds the energy, the formation of the creation of the thought is passed to the subconscious which acts upon the suggestion, offers it to the universe which picks up on the vibration of the energy released and so depending on the strength of this built energy (often created by continued focus and repetition of visiting the same thought over and over) the thought is brought into form and so attracts the very thing focussed upon on that wavelength of vibration. That which is thought with faith and conviction will be delivered. Discipline of mind, practise of positive thought to form a positive outcome with positive vibration is required.

The alignment with soul centre and mind in conjunction will enable purpose of life to materialise, that which mind seeks on the intellectual plane and understood can be found in spiritual core of the individual soul. There is a reason for mind, body and soul. It is a combination which when they are consciously working together true self will be found and be able to unite all three parts in work and play within daily life with the true power of self understood. Individual souls can then move forward in great awareness to fulfil the journey they came to complete and offer service in co-creation with Creator, Source, or God whichever you understand. The divine gifts each individual soul came to earth with being fully utilised and understood.

Mind is complex. It is a part of the co-creation process, it is in part a way to perceive the world of the physical, to determine what is deemed to be real in that particular moment but if it is used in this purpose alone, conscious awareness of a broader realisation that reality is only a perception can be missed. Reality is often not what it seems; there is a bigger picture of why we are here and who we truly are. Mind is only a part of the whole which perceives the world for the soul to experience. An important part but without the realisation of the immortal soul and conscious awareness of this part of your being then there will always be a battle between mind, body and soul.

Belief

We all own patterns of belief which we have been exposed to in our physical reality. We absorb some, are educated in others and acquire some along the road of life experience. Our beliefs limit us to open perspective, to a broader almost incomprehensible, unlimited possibility. We are governed by them and they are what provide us with a boundary within which we choose our next perception and move in life.

Alternatively our belief system can be open, flowing, movable, flexible, open ended offering shifts in our experience and unlimited potentials in our physical reality.

Our belief may be in a particular science, religion, or in nothing at all (that in itself is a chosen belief system) it is all a choice of thought, which determines how we as an individual soul live. Whatever we believe, it stirs us and places us on a particular path. We seek in a particular way within the boundaries of that belief system and so it is that all these patterns are valid, for they are personal choice. They are what we choose for our own path.

We have, however, many possibilities and potentials within our life on earth and this is part of the era of spiritual renaissance when we recognise that we have unlimited potentials not just one path, not just one beginning through to one ending without choice. We always have choice of thought and therefore form and potentials in life.

We may be limited by beliefs about ourselves and so feel stuck in one pattern of behaviour. The freedom is in the realisation that choice is there. Make a better choice, change the belief about self. Get to the root and see what needs to change, potentials are immense when we realise we are in control of our choices and our beliefs about ourselves.

Belief in God, in Source, belief in our connection to that Source and belief in self and that we are unlimited souls in a physical garment, living an earthly experience enables us to see life in a broader perspective. All other choices of belief can lie within this system. If we are aware when we are limiting ourselves, be it in our inner dialogue regarding our health or if we are deciding we cannot achieve something, then if we see this in conscious awareness we know we can change the thought immediately. We can see that one new thought followed by belief and faith, a knowing that the situation is already changed, then adding energy to this belief offers a new potential outcome. In accepting this new potential with full belief knowing it is already on its way to you then you change the outcomes in your life. By doing this you are using conscious living with conscious awareness of your own belief system constantly shifting it to give the best outcome and offer unlimited potentials. This is conscious living, allowing conscious awareness.

Your belief system about yourself, your family, your friends, your relationships, your world around you, who you are in life, your status, who you really are have formed over a lifetime but where you feel limited, stuck or feel there is no way forward check your belief systems around these situations and as suggested create a new potential, go to the root. Is it fear? Be honest with yourself, your belief system and see if you can move this into a different potential outcome. You have the gift to do so. It is a matter of belief in self and your divine connection.

There is a system for all to use but we often choose to stay in the focus of the problem and our belief in that problem becomes greater. We need to focus on the solution and how good that feels. We need to see that we are the answer to our problems and this is the gift God, Source, Creator has given us to use.

We have forgotten who we are. We believe in something outside of ourselves and look to that for our solution. There is something higher than ourselves but we have a part of that within us and so this is how we can co-create and change our outcomes in life. We have to see, to have belief in this something within us, a divine connection and use it to our benefit when we get stuck, when we can only see the problem.

We are capable of shifting the immovable obstacle with a review of our belief system. We can ask for healing and guidance, or we can choose a better thought, offer something in service to others, raise our energy, and see the solution. Have belief in us, ourselves, our own power and with dignity and divine connection move forwards. Believe.

Wisdom

Many teachers have come to the earth over many centuries and offered pathways to understanding of life on earth. Wisdom over the centuries has been hidden and passed on in riddles and legends to protect those who would carry the message in the hope that it would be understood later in time. Perhaps waiting for a new era when ancient teachings and new beginnings coincide and come together to enrich the understanding of humanity.

Many texts, scrolls and other dimensional teachings have yet to be uncovered. In this, the history of humanity will change, for what is believed and already discovered will take on a new meaning when other teachings are added. In this then wisdom from the past can be brought up to date in the future. It is all a matter of understanding of readiness. This guidance is given to help with the understanding that this is a new era of spiritual renaissance; new beginning in understanding the past in context of the evolution of humanity for the future.

Wisdom is an ongoing flow of understanding, the context of evidence mixed with a realisation of self and remembrance of the skills humanity really possesses.

Messengers will continue to bring forth that which was already seen and known but with the new understanding of souls now on earth willing to receive this new and ancient wisdom in order to reveal to all, the power within all humanity, the power of unlimited potential for good, the good of all, to add value and strength to souls of great wisdom.

In ancient times great technologies existed, great psychic and telepathic communications, great sources of unlimited energy existed; however, humanity was both too spiritual and not strong enough to defend against oppressors and so being truly pacifists were destroyed as a community, or some were more of a physical nature and threw off any spiritual side. Balance had been devastated. Remnants survived but skills were diluted and forgotten or protected by the few for another time. Alternative populations were without these skills and were operating on a lower level of energy frequency and so skills were protected and humanity has evolved in some respects now to be able to understand what the implications are of having conscious awareness of such skills and the responsibility that goes with them.

There is a need for a spiritual renaissance to protect the earth and evolve humanity once more away from devastation. There is a need to understand there are skills from ancient times which can be passed on now to many, who are waiting to receive from messengers who are willing to pass on wisdom from such times. In understanding the mysteries of the past we can help to evolve the earth and its people to a higher frequency, ultimately one of peace and tranquillity.

We are ready to reveal these wisdoms at the time when it is right to receive, we believe many, not all just yet, but many on earth are strong enough to understand and this is important, responsible enough to hold knowledge and use the knowledge in a way which will benefit the earth rather than use it for reward.

Wisdom of the past will be revealed in many different ways: translated from scripts and decoded, moved from recesses where secrets of the past have been hidden. The time is approaching when the lessons from the centuries gone, the advancements of technology and a spiritual seeking or should we say seeing, all comes together to create an opportunity for messages to be brought forward which will help the earthly experience and also benefit Mother Earth herself.

It is time for humanity to awake, to remember who we are, to reclaim our spiritual beginnings and use our true gifts in the true exploration of self, and to hold these gifts close to our hearts to enable evolution which has been long awaited.

These blessings are humanity's gifts and also humanity's responsibilities. There will be great reward for all embracing both these aspects. When humanity has accomplished this task of understanding true self, through ancient and new evolving knowledge then humanity shall have established true wisdom.

Peace

Peace, a simple word yet a hard order to achieve. Let it start with self. Peace in one's heart, peace in your life, in your home, in your being. This will then ripple outwards to your friends, family and further to your new acquaintances.

To attain peace, self-awareness, exploration has to take place. Self-love even your darker weaker parts, embrace them, accept them, heal them with your love, assign your beliefs in the positive and go forward speaking your soul's truth, respecting all others as you go. It is a tall order, yes? Yet it is simply achieved by letting go of all that does not serve you; by feeling a way that is based in faith and conviction in self and the divine connection and relationship with your God in being your highest self and tapping into your own unlimited potential.

Your realisation that you can choose thought, a better thought to co-create a new potential whenever needed. This is the wisdom the ancients knew and many teachers taught us that we have access to true peace.

Peace is in the heart and the right of the soul. It rests in the knowledge that your mind is at rest to enable alignment of purpose and through your subconscious bring into form, that which your body can act out in the physical experience, to add value and serve for benefit of the world in the form of the unique you.

Peace is alignment with soul; it is balance of mind, body, spirit. It is faith, trust, conviction, love and compassion. It is that which we have offered you in understanding in these writings.

Peace is love of humanity, honouring connection with your God, having a deep personal relationship with that God, one to one and co-creating from that standpoint for the benefit of the earth and all her inhabitants.

It is being in connection with your fellow man and treating him as your brother/sister. Peace is self-knowledge, self-love. It is the joy of the little things, also of health, well-being, security, comfort.

It is creating in your God's love all that is needed and it is recognising that there is nothing to fear, that life and learning is continuous and life is constantly evolving.

Peace is following your heart, doing more of what you love and have passion for, ensuring you attempt that which you dream of, then completing it. Peace is service, it is adding value, and it is giving. Peace is in receiving and accepting.

Peace on earth is a potential, a possibility, it is like all thoughts which become form dependent upon faith and conviction. It is how much it is desired, thought about and given focus, faith, conviction and energy to.

Peace is a possibility on earth, it begins with each individual soul and it begins with the work within to manifest without. All form starts with a thought.

Peace is then a conscious awareness of how humanity can recognise and remember who it truly is and its connection to spirit.

Peace begins with resolution of small differences; it begins with the small and expands to the larger picture.

Life can be peaceful; every day can be peaceful. Each start to the day each individual soul can set the intention for the day to be a path of peaceful awareness "I set my peace today" and if it goes astray then choose again to reset your day as you would reset your technology which has a blip in its working. Be consciously aware in this way, constantly revising your thoughts, your choices, your actions, your convictions, until one day there will be no need for revision just vision of who you truly are and how you truly operate to manifest peace and contentment in your life daily.

This is the way of conscious awareness. This is the era of humanity's learning to appreciate its spiritual renaissance.

"Peace is with you always."

Spiritual Evolution

Humanity has undergone many spiritual evolutions and many evolutions in general. This one is another where it is hoped the teachings of the past, religious, scientific, spiritual can be combined in a way which can bring about huge change on the earth and the way in which humanity works with each other.

There is a great seeking within the hearts of people for a new beginning, a soul's longing for change in the way humanity struggles with itself and denies its own birth right. To renew the connection to highest Source and have recognition of its own power of manifestation, not for just small desires within individual lives but a spiritual alchemy where manifestation of a life in peace, love and compassion, in cooperation can be achieved on earth.

A heaven on earth has been spoken of in religious texts and other teachings, "As above so below." This phrase many times misunderstood. The answers are always within. There is a need for understanding, a raising of vibration and conscious awareness in order to raise humanity as a whole to achieve a new level of positive energy. This is part way to the larger goal.

This is a spiritual evolution. It begins of course with individual souls and when their energy is expanding, the vibration of each soul's energy body will be resonating and expand others by being who they are and a ripple effect begins. We all have an energy body; we are more than just the physical body. Mind and body, soul energy are all parts of our being and so the more we are consciously in balance the more we can raise our own frequency.

It is up to individual choice, but in this era of spiritual evolution it has been offered to you. The power of your thoughts is magnificent. Do not fear your magnificence, instead believe in it, have faith in it and go into the world strong to help the world move forward, evolve not just in the physical, medical advancements, not just in the technological advancements but in the spiritual too.

This lack of conscious awareness of power of self is what is holding humanity back from its ultimate resolution of problems on earth. It has developed in many areas but still denies that which is imminent. Not only does it deny it, it ridicules it and throws it aside.

However, now is the time when there is an awakening, an opening in the possibilities of mankind. We cannot express enough the possibilities available within the potential of this renaissance. There will be great rejoicing when mankind has true self-realisation, finds peace within itself and solves its own problems and avoids possibility of devastation.

We stand in faith that the message of spiritual evolution will be received and so enlightenment and uplifting take place with the realisation that all is well and will always be well because mankind wills it to be so. The manifestation on earth of great form of cooperation because of realisation of man's ability to manifest these things in divine faith and conviction will be a wonderful thing to watch.

Life on earth is a magnificent opportunity and none more so than in this era where mankind can achieve complete self-knowledge and spiritual awareness of how the soul, the mind and the body works in harmony with the divine Creator and Mother Earth in a wonderful evolution of mankind.

Humanity has taken a long journey over many thousands of years, millions of years. Many different existences, cultures, religions, communities have walked upon this treasured earth, yet now is the time when all this learning can be accumulated together. All teachings from ancient texts and seemingly new advancements can come together in spiritual alliance with an uplifting and true understanding of your connection to your God. The understanding of how God is connected to human souls in everyday life. The continuous evolution of souls who can connect purpose of soul with the physical reality of everyday life, spreading love, compassion, kindness and knowledge, forming a new way forward for humanity CAN become a reality. It will be a combined spiritual and physical evolution, a living in peace and contentment through an awakened consciousness standpoint.

This is the end of these letters for this time. We bid you peace, contentment, great love and understanding. Be at peace with yourselves and your neighbours. Live your life in full and complete awareness of your full potential and awaken to who you truly are as a unique soul of love and light with a specific purpose for your physical life on earth.

We hold you always in our love.